When You Reach
The End Of Your Rope,
Let Go!

When You Reach
The End Of Your Rope,
Let Go!

Geoffrey Rose, Ph.D.

This book was printed in the United States of America
by FineArts Printing Services 866.480.0550.

To order additional copies of this book, contact:
Awareness Press
5850 West Third Street #304
Los Angeles, CA 90036
awarenesspress@earthlink.net

To Bobbi, Melanie, and Tracey.
You helped me to understand who I was . . .
And who I was no longer.

Contents

PART TWO: From Skeptic to Mystic *108*

Introduction | Read Me First

In order to accomplish any complicated task, I have always found it wise to have a good solid plan, one that has already proven itself to be effective and repeatable. Since the ins and outs of personal transformation can be so dizzyingly complex, I was inspired to write *When You Reach the End of Your Rope, Let Go!* to offer those "on the path" just such a time-tested plan. Here is a simple, straightforward blueprint, a soup-to-nuts "How-to," created specifically to help pry you loose from your current stuck position. Whether you are rooted in fear (worry, doubt, anger, guilt—all forms of fear), or simply "living in your head," (having an analytical rather than an experiential approach to life), *When You Reach the End of Your Rope, Let Go!* is designed to guide you step-by-step until you are emotionally, ideologically, energetically, and *actually* in a new and better place.

Self-help books tend to go in and out of vogue. Our tastes today seem to run more along the lines of having our lessons delivered in colorful vignettes, testimonials, conversations, or beautifully written fables. Don't get me wrong, I love many of these books. But without helping you to develop a fundamentally new perspective, without facilitating access to and release of your subconscious beliefs and emotional blocks, these works remain STs . . . spirit-teasers.

When You Reach the End of Your Rope, Let Go! means to help you shift from a life characterized by doubt and difficulty, to one filled with love, joy, and success. Accomplishing this necessitates a nuts-and-bolts, hands-on approach. The mastery of your inherent mental and spiritual abilities requires a communication far too specific to be left merely to anecdote, nuance, suggestion, or for that matter, faith, no matter how strong. I have set out to deliver the goods as dynamically and as entertainingly as possible, but prepare yourself to flex some new muscles (literally), for true growth can never be attained passively. If you are ready to move from the whimsical to the practical, this book is for you.

When You Reach the End of Your Rope, Let Go! will guide you through a process of discovery and release of your fear-based thinking. In so doing, it means to restore your imagination back to you—the ability to believe what you cannot yet see. This talent, as you will soon discover, is vital to your personal happiness and success. To this end, you will be given a simple, time-saving and energy-efficient tool called *The Emotional Detoxx*. Based on the outstanding work of pioneers in the fields of Applied and Clinical Kinesiology, The Emotional Detoxx (an anagram for **D**isowning **E**very **T**hought **O**ut to Double-cross (**XX**) you) is a powerful, proven method of self-discovery and self-mastery. It is also fun and easy to learn, employing techniques that were specifically designed to expedite your personal evolution.

~ ~ ~

 What has been seriously lacking in the area of self-help is a way for the individual to access his own subconscious mind. As Transpersonal Psychology pioneer Ken Wilber says, "In order to know what is in a mind, you have got to talk to it." You see, if it were simply the physical contents of the brain you were interested in, you could either scan it or cut into it—in some way put it through the rigors of scientific investigation. **But a mind you must communicate with—especially your own. This is precisely why The Emotional Detoxx was created. It is the key reason you have discovered this book and now read these words.**

You will also be introduced to the metaphysical/spiritual

practice I call *Thought Farming*—mind-over-matter made possible. Together, these two tools represent the missing link between you and a better life. With them, you will rediscover your forgotten Self—your repressed feelings and hidden beliefs—particularly those that have kept you fearing, doubting, angsting, and otherwise tiptoeing through what should unabashedly be your life. In so doing, you will wake to a new awareness: *You are infinitely more than you ever suspected.* Conversely, your limited, negative sense of yourself was just someone else's opinion all along, monstrously gone awry, naively forged into personal gospel.

At the outset, I wish to say that this book, as all books, will speak more successfully to some than to others. Those experiencing a psychosis, such as schizophrenia, for example—may not find solace in this work. The Emotional Detoxx and Thought Farming are designed for those of us who stubbornly stand in our own way and know it, but just cannot seem to *do* anything about it. These tools are ideally suited for those members of that obstinate majority I fondly call the "garden-variety neurotics."

Though many may find benefit from The Emotional Detoxx and Thought Farming, it is the veteran seeker who is apt to gain the most. *When You Reach the End of Your Rope, Let Go!* will speak the loudest to those who have "had it up to here" with the labyrinthine nature of talk-therapy . . . But anyone may hear.

~~~

In addition to the dramatic results made possible through the revolutionary approach to personal growth within these pages, it is the combination and integration of these special techniques with the metaphysical aspects of the work that I believe will make this a truly successful, transformative personal growth system for you. Without a spiritual context, all therapy—self-administered or otherwise—is a lot like rearranging the deck chairs on the Titanic. No matter where you put what, you are going down.

Without a practical understanding of metaphysical or spiritual law, or a first-hand experience of one's own divine nature, even the most dedicated seeker will continue to "take on the water" of fear and self-doubt and eventually sink under the weight of their ongoing personal misgivings. My hope is that by employing both a scientific and a spiritual approach to your situation, you will finally be able to "connect the dots," and, at last, get a realistic, hopeful, and workable picture of yourself. A good likeness would, indeed, insist upon it.

~~~

When You Reach the End of Your Rope, Let Go! is a pilgrimage of mind/body/spirit consciousness. It is a new route, cutting through the seemingly fearful and hazardous terrain of your old misguided thoughts and jagged emotions. It is offered to you with the greatest love, the deepest respect, and the strongest conviction that here is the least circuitous path yet forged on the way from the promise of a better life to that promise fulfilled.

At its best, this book will serve as a guide forward to a more aware, unencumbered, spirit-based way of living. Once you arrive here, every moment will hold the magic of possibility, unfettered by self-limiting prejudice, deception, or doubt. My hope is that these pages will also jog the primordial memory of a forgotten personal paradise and, in so doing, help you to give consent to a more complete and more satisfying experience of yourself.

Lastly, it is my wish that these words find resonance within you and that they speed you on your way in this, the most noble of all possible causes—the reclamation of your truly remarkable Self.

Author's Note: You will notice that within the text I refer to both God and Thought Farmers as "He." I apologize in advance for this choice, for in no way do I wish to deliberately "genderize" either. For better or worse, it still seems the most universally accepted approach to this dilemma.

Additionally, if you are pregnant or nursing it might be wise for you to hold off doing the exercises herein. Strange as this might sound, emotional toxicity is real, and there is no way for us to know with absolute certainty that its release into and then out of your system would not in some way affect your child. Better safe than sorry.

Finally, throughout the book you will find twelve "secrets" and twelve exercises. Consider each "secret" as you discover it. You could handle the exercises in this fashion as well or you might prefer to wait until you have finished reading the book in its entirety before doing them. There are no rules. Also, a second reading of the material might be warranted before approaching the exercises if what is presented here is either challenging to you or difficult for you to accept.

Part One: The Beginning . . .

A Very Scary Place To Start

Letting go requires courage and wisdom . . .
Courage to transcend your fears,
Wisdom to transcend your beliefs.

-1- | Me

I was born on the verge of a nervous breakdown . . . Then things got worse. I was taught by example that the world was a frightening, inhospitable place. Because of this, and because I instinctively knew that I was a part of that world, and it a part of me, I mistakenly assumed that I could not trust myself either.

As a toddler, I developed severe allergies. So while friends began acquiring dogs and cats as pets, skepticism and self-hate were fast becoming my constant companions. Like many of my clients, by the time I had the wherewithal to get myself into therapy, I could not remember ever feeling anything but "bad."

Seven years of various forms of psychotherapy preceded eight years of psychoanalysis. Fifteen frustrating years of one type of therapy after the next, from Gestalt to Freudian, yet I was still dependent on that weekly visit. Something was definitely wrong with *that* picture. Psychotherapy had become just one more compensation for the terrible sense of "lack" that had always and still lived within me. There had to be a way to break the cycle of fear, resentment, and self-doubt and to champion myself in the life of which I had always suspected myself capable. There was, and herein I share that discovery with you.

~~~

Because of my emotionally inauspicious beginnings, it became an instant interest of mine to seek "happiness." It is only when we are hungry that we go hunting. I was a born hunter. I became a meditator in my early twenties, but had begun psychotherapy years before that—somewhere in my pre-teens—having reduced myself to a stuttering, bed-wetting, head-banging, peptically ulcerated, obsessive/compulsive asthmatic. I was a mess. Self-hate was crippling me; self-confidence—just an oxymoron.

What was needed, in my case, was an extensive emotional clearing before any intention, focus, or ambition could be entertained, or before any motivational work could begin in earnest. On top of all this, I was born and raised with my identical twin brother, Sam. Now, Sam's a great guy, but having to share an identity with him for the first twenty or so years of my life threw another major wrench into the works.

I share this blistery history with you, not because I enjoy rummaging through yesterday's garbage, but because I want you to feel secure in the knowledge that the author of a book on breakdown, breakthrough, and personal evolution has successfully run the gauntlet. Throughout *When You Reach the End of Your Rope, Let Go!*, I offer details of my own struggle with decades of depression, doubt, and disease, because mine is a universal story, and it may give hope to the reader who finds him- or herself in short supply.

Now, let's talk about you . . . .

-2- | You

Your ruts may be awful, but they are awfully familiar. The prospect of a brave new world of love, prosperity, joy, and abundance, as attractive as it may *sound*, is frighteningly *unfamiliar*. You will, if you are truly interested in bettering your life, have to forfeit—let go—your old worn-out ways and belief systems. This takes genuine desire and great courage. Only you know how badly you want a better life. The more passionate you are about this, the more certain you will be of success. If you can approach what follows with an open mind, your historic reluctance to change may soon be a thing of the past.

You are nobody's fool. If anything, you may even have had the thought that you are probably just a little too smart to ever *really* be happy. You have read book after book, all touting the endless benefits of living your life according to spiritual principle. And if intelligence had anything to do with it, or if joyful, healthful, successful living could have been learned vicariously or through osmosis, you would have gotten it by now. So far, though, you have come away empty-handed, save for the growing conviction that there is something remarkable "out there" ... some slippery, all-too-elusive Truth ... some golden key somewhere, so close. But you cannot find it, cannot hold it in your hands or use its surefire magic to unlock the universe's golden treasure chest of shimmering love, joy, health, and prosperity.

Indeed, metaphysically based material of all kinds is making its mystical way in ever-greater supply onto the nightstands of a vast and hopeful readership. But, sadly, all too few of us get any real benefit from these would-be "magical" messages, and the promise that has slept in our hearts since before we can remember still sleeps.

With all the wisdom that is virtually exploding out of the dark recesses of what only a few years ago would have been dismissed as "the occult," you still find yourself just too ill-prepared—emotionally, spiritually, and psychologically—to take advantage of even the most basic health, happiness, or prosperity principles. Why? Because you, as you now realize yourself, are the product of misinformation—negative societal and genetic imprinting. Therefore you are unlikely to suddenly jettison your anger, fear, or skepticism simply because you are now being told (in no uncertain terms) that it is absolutely, unquestionably, beyond any shadow of a doubt in your own best interest.

~~~

It is not for want of information that you suffer. You know that *love is the answer.* Everyone from Christ to the Beatles to Oprah has shared this basic truth with you. But where is love? It is blind, we say, and so cannot find us. Then, there is the notion of tithing, based on the well-known spiritual axiom: *Give and your gift shall be returned to you ten-fold.* But generosity, too, stubbornly remains an unlearned lesson. Having an attitude of gratitude—giving thanks—is spiritually fundamental, and indeed it stands as one of the best practical ways of increasing supply. *To have more tomorrow, we must be grateful today.* Uh-huh . . . sure, but we just can't seem to get with *that* program either. And finally . . . *you reap what you sow.* Absolutely! You've heard this truism your whole life. But changing your crop thus far has seemed all but impossible.

~~~

Ultimately you lack something other than knowledge; you lack *the appreciation of who you actually are.* It is my privilege to bring you the news that you are a remarkable creation. You can dramatically improve the quality of your life by learning the truth of this, and by letting go of your old unworkable self-concepts. Herein you will find some new tools for accomplishing this—practical tools for living in the Here and Now . . . and happily ever after.

As a child, you were promised a world filled with magic. Well, believe it or not, your life *can* be like a fairy tale. But a working appreciation of this does not happen *to* you, it happens *through* you. You are about to join, in the words of Neale Donald Walsch, author of *Conversations with God*, the "evolution revolution." You are about to embark on a journey of conscious evolution —an evolution of your consciousness—a journey that will, when all is said and done, lead you home again.

-3- | There's No Place Like "OM"

The road back to your actual, happy, healthy "Self"—the individual, idiosyncratic you that still longs to be recognized, welcomed, and celebrated—is a journey that should be far more adventurous than arduous. As ironic as it may seem, and as far away from your goal as you may now feel, you have never actually left the "place" you seek. Like Dorothy in *The Wizard of Oz*, your "somewhere over the rainbow place" has been in your own backyard all along.

What may seem even more fantastic than the analogy this powerful metaphysical children's story provides, is the realization that this "over the rainbow place" actually lies within you, that it is, in fact, *you*. The "road" home to yourself only seems to wander endlessly hither and yon, as you stagger side-to-side, lost within your own beliefs and emotions.

One reason you probably "misplaced" yourself was because your parents wielded enormous influence over you— their collective voice drowning out the sound of your own. That is natural. But if you consciously or subconsciously continue to buy into your parent-driven self-limiting concepts, or create new beliefs through an unconscious filtering of that which does not fit your old established status quo "reality," you are doomed to endlessly suffer prejudicial and predictable results.

This dislocation from yourself—leading to disorientation, the acceptance of blame, and the abandonment of your worth—is the beginning of the end of any hope that you may ever have had for personal happiness. Your parents, indeed, would have seemed all great and powerful to your young, inexperienced eyes, ears, and heart; so why don't you just chalk the whole thing up to an honest mistake, and get on with the business of self-reparation.

~~~

Fortunately, the experience you seek already exists deep within you, whispering softly to your every sense. Haven and heaven, it hides, as Deepak Chopra, M.D., likes to say, in the silence between your thoughts. This energetic "place" also happens to be the real land of make believe, where, when all is said and done, only those who believe that *they* make their lives may enter it. It is the world of "Om," the sound used in contemplating ultimate reality through meditation. You must be very still, though it is within and around you every moment—entrance to this enchanting kingdom, or queendom, must await your turning the esoteric keys of self-recognition, self-acceptance, and self-transcendence.

You have the power to affect enormous change in your world, to wield far greater influence over your destiny than any other person who has ever lived. Your potential is immense, but your power is only yours, if you accept it. Now is the time for you to wake and take advantage of your substantial, albeit conditional gifts.

~~~

Unfortunately, most of us are looking for some sort of wizard—someone wiser than us—someone to show us the way "home." Like Dorothy in *The Wizard of Oz*, we will go to great lengths to find such a person. Maybe we can learn something from Dorothy's experience. What did *her* wizard do? If you recall, in his speech to Dorothy and her friends, Professor Marvel offers each character a symbolic representation of their "missing" quality.

He hands the Lion—a medal, the Tin Man—a "heart," and the Scarecrow—a diploma. This seems to work a small miracle, making all the difference in the world to these colorful characters, these fictional emotional counterparts of ourselves. Even though his hoax and true identity are eventually revealed, Professor Marvel is still able to work his wizardry. Perhaps he really is a wizard after all, or maybe he just knows something that our frightened friends do not ... *He knows that* **recognition** *is the key that unlocks the door to our potential.*

~~~

As children, we needed this recognition to come from the outside. As adults, it must come from within. The only true wizard in your world happens to be you. One would think that would be good news. But all too often, we cast our parents in the Wizard's role. And, just as in Dorothy's story, our parents, whose God-like power comes closest to approaching the Wizard's status in our lives, must also be exposed for the impostors (false-gods) that they are. Like the Wizard, they too, are just people. And, as in the story, even though parents ultimately must be exposed as the frightened men and women that they are—each hiding behind his or her own "curtain"—it is still powerfully good to be recognized by them.

More importantly, as with the Lion, the Scarecrow, and the Tin Man, you, too, already possess the very qualities you hunger for. All roads do indeed lead home, yellow brick or otherwise, even those that take a detour somewhere over the rainbow. Look to yourself. Trust no would-be wizards.

~~~

To drive the point even further home, we learn that the secret to Dorothy's return trip to Kansas has also been with *her* all along—these, the ruby red slippers. And what magic words must she say, what witch's incantation must she utter to spirit herself back to her beloved Kansas? "There's no place like home . . . there's no place like home . . . ." If it weren't so true, it would be nauseatingly hokey. Nevertheless, all four of our heroes learn the very same lesson: that everything they ever needed or wanted was already there inside them, "right in their own back yards."

You must learn, by all means available to you, to think your own thoughts, Scarecrow; to rise to your natural courage, Lion; and to trust your own beautiful heart, Tin Man. Everything you ever hoped you could be, you already are. It has always been right there—inside you—right where you were all along.

There is a memory you may have from childhood that might help convince you of this . . . .

-4- | Forward Into the Past

Can you recall the frightened, anxious feelings that swept through you the first time you climbed onto a bicycle, and shook and teetered back and forth, unable to go in any direction but sideways and down? The bike looked so beautiful, so shiny and inviting—promising speed, freedom, and independence. But behind its beauty and promise lay its dark side. It was so big, so unmanageably awkward . . . even dangerous. Oh, but you wanted to ride so badly. The desire was so great that you were willing to try over and over again—to challenge your fear—each time travelling just a little bit further . . . till the inevitable tumble came. Undaunted, you would climb right back on, and try it again . . . and again . . . and again.

You knew that it could be done, perhaps because you had seen the other kids doing it. Or maybe it was because your skepticism was still in its infancy. Either way, your *spirit* and imagination became fused with a sort of divine expectancy. Now it was just a matter of figuring out "how." Not simply with your *mind*, though. A lot of this calculating had to be done with your *body*. No amount of theorizing alone was going to get you to confidently, then eventually even brazenly, leap onto those two wheels and barrel down the road into your adolescence. Your muscles, indeed the very cells of your body needed practice, practice experiencing themselves in brand new ways. And that practice required repetition—the mother of *all* learning. You needed, unbeknownst to you, what is called "body knowledge"— to carve out new neuronal pathways in your brain and to develop additional avenues of communication between it and the rest of you.

So, practice you did, your desire never waning. Convinced that it could be done, you did not give up. And soon you were up and riding, and feeling, if you can recall, pretty darn good about yourself. You see, your brain (the Scarecrow), your heart (the Tin Man), and your courage (the Lion) all pulled together rather beautifully, offering you a powerful win.

~~~

Much in the same way that you learned to ride that first bike of yours—through a deliberate, conscious intention and the unbridled mastery of physical balance—you can learn—through a mastery of *metaphysical* balance and an intention reclaimed and reconstituted—to alter the very nature of what has been running you—your earliest acquired belief imprints. You must, however, first unlearn much before you will be ready to create your life anew. But just as soon as this de-education is underway, Spirit—your Spirit—will have a chance to stretch out and to reengage Itself. Once you are deliberately and consciously spirit-based, having distinguished yourself from your thought, you may then *retrain your habitual imaginings* to favor what you desire, rather than, as has historically been the case, what you fear.

To get back on track, you will first want to retrace and correct your ideological and emotional misguided steps, and recognize and examine your "knee-jerk" thoughts and feelings. This requires the discovery and release of "negative" body-conscious material—repressed emotion—which will then lead to the "let go," the relaxing and surrendering into what is left . . . You—heretofore the Great Unknown.

~~~

So there *is* a passage back to the golden fields of your early optimism, full health, and unlimited potential. And though you may doubt it, and the idea of backtracking through your thorny emotional underbrush may seem to you treacherous at best, in so many ways this is a far more beautiful journey than you could ever imagine.

We may ask ourselves, "Where has the courage and passion of childhood gone? How is it that fear, not exuberance, now seems the dominant player in our lives?" Reaching the end of our rope and letting go is ultimately about recovering our true Selves, our natural desire, and the all-important conviction, "I *can* do that."

You may not have realized it at the time, but as you energetically drifted from your hopeful beginnings, you left yourself a belief "bread crumb trail"—sort of like Hansel and Gretel. You crafty little devil, you. Ah, but you are going to need great courage, a healthy helping of desire, and the acquisition of a few good new skills before you will be able to follow it back. When you do, it will lead you out of that fearful yet all too familiar place in which you currently live. Out of that endless sameness from which you cannot seem to extricate yourself. Out of your witch's kitchen, where you have been cooking up a lifetime of image-based, fear-based, self-sabotaging behavior.

After you have ushered "her" into her own oven, and have set out on your way home again, your days will suddenly seem a lot brighter. And you will find that getting out of bed in the morning, an event that may now require great leverage, will become something that you actually look forward to doing.

~ ~ ~

When you wake to the understanding that it is your perception that defines your experience (and that where there is deception there is *misperception* and proportionately that much less joy, growth, and success), you realize that uncovering self-deceit becomes key to the redemption of your value, the continuation of your personal evolution, and the subsequent return of your lost joy. Once undertaken, vanquishing duplicity proves a psychological, emotional, and spiritual quest—a quest that must, at times, feel, and indeed be, rather solitary. Though it goes without saying, I will say it anyway: where there is no longer duplicity ("twoness"), there really can be only one Thing . . . Oneness—You—*sans* gurus, *sans* any "outside" authority whatsoever.

Yes, I believe in *some* therapy. I believe in *some* therapists. Heaven knows I have certainly had my share. But above all, I believe in the individual, and the God-given personal authority that, when exercised, must ultimately lead you out of your therapist's office forever. If you are not in touch with this authority, then you are a victim of deception—a hoax perhaps not originally of your design, but now assuredly of your maintenance.

One of your most important new skills, therefore, will involve the long-awaited ability to differentiate between yourself and your old misguided beliefs—your self-deceptions. The power of thought must be understood. And the ability to delineate between the thought and the thinker, a must.

What we nurture in ourselves will grow.
That is nature's eternal law.

Goethe

-5- | What the Heck Is Thought Farming?

For many years, I have had the fantasy of creating a more joyful, healthier, naturally more "connected" way of living. The picture of this in my mind has always been the same . . . .

I live on a beautiful farm, nestled among rolling foothills, somewhere deep in the heart of God's country. I am far away both in miles and mentality from the turbulent city life I know so well.

I rise with the sun, because this is what I choose to do. I set about my daily chores with a light heart, a full spirit, and hands strengthened by good, honest work. I am happy to be alive.

I understand Nature, and work alongside It in awe and admiration. I have a deep respect for all life, which I understand in some way to be connected to my own.

I am not afraid. I know that everything has a purpose, and that if I become frightened it is only because I am unaware of that purpose.

I do not begrudge the crow its flight nor the deer its freedom, simply because it is their nature to feed in my fields. I will, however, do what I can to protect my crop till harvest.

Living with me on the farm are many different kinds of animals. I enjoy the variety of their character and temperament, and I am never bored.

By nightfall, the day's work has left me exhausted, yet my spirit, mind, and body are strengthened by what I was able to accomplish through my efforts today. I am humbled by a life of endless grace. I sleep the sleep of angels . . . .

No way. I know myself too well. I could never really be happy with this rural rough-and-ready life. It sounds tempting, but before you could say "Old MacDonald," I would miss the bright lights of the big city and be chomping at the proverbial bit for just the slightest whiff of bus exhaust.

What is it, then, that my soul seems so hungry for, if it is not the physical lifestyle of the farmer itself? Perhaps it is the simple, direct, no-nonsense way he appears to move through life, that holds this strange, mystical power over me. Throughout the years, as I continued to search within and for myself, I discovered that this was indeed the case. I realize now that this yearning for a simpler, more connected way of living is my inheritance—the karmic whisperings of untold generations before mine. The message is that there is a better way, a healthier, more sustaining and sustainable way to live with myself, my fellow humans, and the earth.

And so, it is this hands-on, Nature-savvy, deliberate approach to living life that sets the tempo and the tone for the creative process I now call Thought Farming. If I would not take myself to the farm, I would bring the farm to me.

-6- | Life Mirrors Consciousness: Thought Farming As Poetic Justice

We are all Thought Farmers. Only a handful of us know it. Men, women, and children, we work God's hours—perpetually planting one thing or another in the fertile ground of our "potential." Here, out in the sprawling fields of possibility, you and I grow our lives; our bodies and outer physical world finding root in the inner realm of thoughts and feelings. *We harvest what we plant with our attitude and intention.*

This is fundamental Thought Farmer wisdom. It has been called the Law of Correspondence: "As within, so without." Essentially, this makes Thought Farming, whether you realize it or not, your principal occupation.

Thought Farmers, to put it simply, grow life experience. We "till our fields" through imagination and impassioned courses of action, creating (through the Law of Attraction), each and every life experience according to its psycho-energetic roots. Though Thought Farming is very simple work, success is by no means guaranteed. This requires a keen sense of purpose. Without purpose, enthusiasm is in short supply. And without enthusiasm, there is little reason to pay much attention to the "cock-a-doodle-dooing" of our digital, snooze alarm equipped electric "roosters."

Thought Farming is a most efficient and effective way to grow back a lost quality of life, or cultivate a new one. But, as with any enterprise, diligence must be taken. The "topsoil," what we call *mind*, needs to be properly prepared, and our choice of "crop," what we call *thought*, must take into account the nature of the "land," what we call *spirit*. To everything, there is a season: knowing when to plant; when to let nature do its work; and knowing when to harvest is essential. Finally, we will need to understand the basics of all farming. Simply put (once more with feeling): *We reap what we sow.* Yes, indeed, Christ was most definitely a Thought Farmer.

~~~

The life of the Thought Farmer is rich and rewarding. He lives close to the earth, knowing the great connection between himself and all things. He is enthusiastic, because he knows that by the sweat of his brow and the focus of his intention, he can grow almost anything. He need only follow natural law and work diligently.

Thought Farming can be a dirty job. Working out in the "field" all day long can get pretty messy. But he does not mind. The Thought Farmer understands that sometimes, if he is to get what he really wants, he might have to get down into the mud. That's O.K. with him. He knows it will wash off.

If his inner "ground"—his general mood, attitude, and overall emotional state—has become depleted or hardened, he will need to spend some time nursing it back to health. This is the job of The Emotional Detoxx. He must not resent this. It is just part of being a conscientious Thought Farmer.

~~~

As alike as we Thought Farmers can be, no two of us are ever exactly the same. What you decide to plant in your "field" is likely to be quite different from what I choose to plant in mine. You are you and I am me, and that is good. The world requires great diversity to sustain itself in balance and integrity.

The writer might consider her ideal harvest to be a well-turned phrase; the heart surgeon—probably a successful bypass or valve replacement; the lawyer—freeing his client from the jaws of injustice; the mother or father—a healthy, happy child.

Unfortunately, most of us were never shown the proper, most effective growing techniques. In fact, back on the family farm, things were run pretty haphazardly. There, suppression was frequently exercised, inhibiting natural expression. In so many ways this left us—the young, inexperienced farmhands—ill equipped, wrestling with the problem of our poor negative attitudes. We just cannot seem to figure out why we should bother doing any of our chores. Heck, they'll all just be back again tomorrow.

Well, if we are to save the farm, we'd best go back to square-one, and come up with some darn good reasons for getting out of our warm beds in the morning.

-7-   The Buck Stops Here

Enthusiasm, joy, spontaneity, and unconditional love, these are the charismatic companions of a healthy human being. *They* might help us shake the sleep from our eyes in the now groggy grey mornings. Unfortunately, many of us were never given much cause to frequent these feelings. It does seem a bit much to ask of parents who were themselves poorly raised. This, it turns out, is key to two critical aspects of self-help. One, our parents, typically, were miserably ill prepared to do any better a job for us than they did (hence, we have a problem). Two, if number one is true, then we must finally stop hoping for better care, attention, love, etc. from *them*, and begin to care for ourselves (hence, the stirrings of a solution). Putting these conditions into motion, "them" becomes "anyone but you." When we do not receive proper nurturing as children, we often turn to others, almost *any* other, in hopes of finally getting our unmet needs satisfied. This must end.

~ ~ ~

When we cease our outward search, and begin turning within, we start to realize how it is that we are in active partnership with the universe. We see that there are no victims, least of all us. And we realize that, even if not always apparent, the same life-rules apply to everyone, equally. Soon we know that what we create in life, we do so by virtue of our conscious and subconscious belief energy. We get out of life what we energetically put into it.

Beliefs based in early life conditions, and even our genetic memory, can, of course, greatly affect this process, both positively and negatively. Getting at and then renegotiating this information becomes especially crucial to the creation of our happiness, when and if this early data proves saboteur. Since much of your time and energy is going to be devoted to dealing with the very real, yet invisible inner dimension of Mind or Consciousness, you-as-Thought Farmer will need only work a small plot of land. This land is the "inner ground" upon which you establish your footing in life and from which you grow yourself, your experiences, and your life conditions. You will not require great acreage, but you will need to dig deep.

~~~

Science has shown that substituting one idea for another actually alters the chemical make-up of the brain, thereby changing our perception of what we call "reality." Many of us have experienced one such alteration of consciousness after buying a new car. Suddenly, we begin to see our car—model and year—everywhere on the road, where before we had hardly noticed it. This type of "attraction" is actually the inevitable result of what is more popularly known as selective perception.

When we buy a new car, let's say a Volvo, we mysteriously and quite suddenly become aware of all the other Volvos on the road. By owning the Volvo we set up an inner resonance that, through a sort of sympathetic vibration, clues us into all the other Volvos. The beliefs we "own" do much the same thing. They draw our attention like magnets draw metal filings. This focus creates a certain "vibration," which then attracts its corresponding physical counterpart. The problem with belief in general is that it narrows the field of possibilities, leaving the lion's share of potential experience unnoticed and unavailable. We must, therefore, exercise great care when choosing and accepting what to believe in.

Even if we put aside this curious sort of "evidence," most of us intuitively understand that our beliefs and our "reality" are inextricably linked. Like the car that we have just bought, what we "own" in consciousness—that which we say *is*—alters what we perceive and, thereby, what we experience.

~~~

Though prevailing wisdom holds that our perception of the world largely dictates our experience within it, the overwhelming majority of us are still unsuccessful in our attempts to change how or what we think and feel. I am sure it is extremely frustrating for you to realize that your beliefs are getting in the way of your happiness, and then to feel either totally powerless or, at the very least, skeptical that you could alter the course of this thinking. Know, however, that any inability or reluctance on your part to change what is not working for you simply indicates that you are still laboring under old misguided beliefs and unresolved emotional issues.

So . . . if there is a reason, then there is a remedy.

Mystic Secret 1: In the Mind, **interpretation equals reality.** Any evolution and every ambition, *any change*, must lead with an evolution of consciousness.

Exercise 1: We need to start weeding our mind gardens. If we want to change how we feel, what we think, and what we are manifesting in our lives, we have got to "tune" our awareness as one sets one's "scope" for finding weeds in a garden. We need to set these scopes of ours and be diligent about identifying our belief "weeds"; those are the interpretations we make that suck up all our energies, leaving us with little or nothing to feed the more desirable, more beautiful "flowers" (thoughts, feelings, and conditions) that we would rather be growing. To help set your scope, suggest the following to yourself and say it *out loud* ten times first thing in the morning and ten times again at bedtime. It will help you to tune your awareness into the "frequency" of your nonbeneficial thought. Simply say and repeat, *"I am now aware of my limiting beliefs . . . ."* In so doing, you will be knocking on the first of your hidden doors. In advancing personal evolution, awareness precedes all deliberate movement. Your consent to that awareness must precede even this. You will soon be given a remarkable tool for accessing the hidden nonbeneficial beliefs within you. This exercise will help prepare you for the full use of it.

Being aware of your thoughts and feelings is always a good idea, especially if they do not support you or the things you say you want. Consider this: Is an ostrich more or less safe having stuck its head in the sand?

	Don't Confuse Me
-8-	With the Facts . . .
	Selective Perception
	Vs. Reality

Mind Truth: Beliefs become automatic self-hypnotic energy delivery devices. Henry Ford, founder of the Ford Motor Car Company, once said, "Whether you believe you can or you believe you can't, you're right." "Reality," you see, is merely the natural manifestation, the mean sum of your beliefs—your intent.

Your beliefs are immensely powerful because you base all your expectations and actions upon them. They are your most vital personal resources, dogmatically relied upon as fact, despite the fact that they were just someone else's opinion, naively taken on faith. Faith, subsequently, proves an unreliable ally that has a dark, libelous side, especially when what you believe is nonsupportive or nonbeneficial to you.

Fortunately, thoughts do not instantly harden into physical form and "pop" full-blown into your experience. Thank God or we would all be in a lot of trouble. But a preponderance of thought, energetically aimed at or in the vicinity of a goal or target (whether desirable or not), will hit that target by creating the experience of it *internally*. Then, through the Law of Correspondence, you will attract like conditions, *externally* (like all those Volvos). The "reality" so generated seems genuine enough, so much so that you may be tempted to think of it as "actuality." But you must not be deceived.

All your circumstances, including your financial conditions, career, personal life, and health (or lack thereof), as real as they seem, are simply temporarily solidified aspects of an otherwise amorphous, malleable field of possibility.

Do not be intimidated by what may initially appear complicated or complex. As with the car that you drive, you need not understand the workings of a combustion engine to get yourself to the supermarket. So, too, it is with the Laws governing the act of creation. You do not need to understand them to "drive" them, either. In fact, you are already driving them, though having your share of "fender benders," I am sure. For whether you understand these Laws or not, they are always at work. The trick is to become conscious of them. And just as in learning to successfully drive a car (or ride that first bike of yours), in learning to *deliberately* create what you desire, you will need to gain a degree of dexterity. This takes practice, just like parallel parking.

~~~

Beliefs, for better or worse, will put blinders on you. If you live haunted by self-doubt and fear, you are an unwitting Johnny Appleseed, sowing the seeds of your eminent disappointment and unhappiness. To belabor an already overly trodden metaphor: As the developing oak *must* follow the "blueprint" within the acorn; depression, anxiety, and a host of compensatory personality disorders and debilitating physical conditions are sure to sprout from the ground of your negative self-talk. It could not be otherwise.

So . . . plant an acorn, grow an oak. If it is an apple tree that you are after, you had better find an apple seed to plant. It is just the same with beliefs and their corresponding conditions. Changing what you reap from your life absolutely requires that you alter what you plant with your mind—your beliefs. By removing the "weeds" of your old disharmonic thoughts and resisted emotions, you ready yourself for a new harvest.

| # Emotional Pretzels And The Fashion Faux Pas

Tolerance for emotional pain proves an important piece of the healing puzzle, and it differs greatly from person to person. What passes for comfort in one may be unbearable to another, as our coping mechanisms vary wildly in their ability to "thicken our skins." How willing you are to change your old unsuccessful ways of thinking and acting will typically be in indirect proportion to how much emotional or physical pain you can tolerate.

You will either experience this pain directly (if you can admit your feelings to yourself) or, having factored in a certain amount of avoidance or denial, find evidence of imbalance—in either your personal or professional life and/or in your health. In either case, how "off" things seem will play a major role in whether you decide to give yourself the opportunity to experience something new (the uncomfortable, progressive choice) or continue along your old course of thought and action (the "comfortable," non-progressive choice). The following anecdote may shine a little light on the nature of this crossroad.

~~~

There is an old Jewish joke about a man who goes to the tailor to be fitted for a new suit. When he returns to pick up the finished garment, the man asks if he might try it on to make certain of the fit. As he stands before the mirror, the man notices that one sleeve is much shorter than the other is. When confronted with his poor workmanship, the tailor bristles, "There's nothing wrong with the suit. You see, if you tuck your arm up into your hip like so, the fit is just perfect." Next, the man notices that one pant leg is much too short. "Well," snaps the tailor, "You just need to bend the one leg a bit."

Unsure of this arrangement, the man decides to live with the suit for a few days before further complaint. As he hobbles out of the tailor's shop, two women pass him in the street. "Did you see that poor, disfigured man," the one says to the other. "Yes," she replies, "but did you notice how handsomely he was dressed?"

~ ~ ~

You and I *are* this man. We have contorted ourselves for years, acclimating to, and then accommodating, the ill-fitting "suits" society and our tailoring parents have styled for us, just so that we, too, might "look good." As silly as it seems that the man in the story would actually consider living with his misfit outfit even for a moment, we must admit to ourselves that we have made just such a choice. We continue our futile efforts to adapt to external expectations, twisting ourselves inside and out with our pretzel-shaped logic. This is done either in hope of being loved and accepted, or to satisfy our demand for comfort, that limited amount afforded us by keeping the old familiar suit on.

Neither image-based nor fear-based decisions, no matter how old or comfortable they are, will ever, *can* ever, lead you to the joyful life you are capable of living. You can continue to hobble around, accommodating your ill-fitting idea suits, thinking somehow that "familiarity" and "joy" are synonyms; or you can take a good look in the mirror. The day that you stand before your own reflection, survey the wreckage, recognize the lunacy, the constriction, the contorted testament to Self-betrayal which you have become—the day that you finally say, "What am I *doing* to myself? This is *ridiculous*"—that day you just might reach the end of *your* rope.

Erik H. Erikson, Pulitzer Prize winning author and leading figure in the field of human development, said that *change always requires the abandonment of the familiar.* Getting "friendly" with this disquieting bit of truth becomes one of your first goals if you are sincere about bettering your life. You notice I do not say that you ought to get "comfortable" with it. As you evolve, you will find that comfort becomes more of an impediment to growth, for it asks that you stay with what is familiar. If you have historically required a great deal of comfort, consider the notion of learning to feel comfortable while poised on the edge of uncertainty. Expect some nervous "butterflies." You are going places that you have never been to before. And expect some beautiful butterflies, too. For you are in the midst of a great metamorphosis.

Throughout your Emotional Detoxx, you will discover a host of "dark" energies—those that have served thus far only to impinge upon and limit the full use of your natural potential. Until you have released the multitudinous libelous messages buried in your subconscious body/mind, and literally detach yourself from them, your life will, unfortunately, reflect the lack and/or limitation that they energetically demand.

When you no longer identify yourself as a repository for unwanted belief and learn to rise above the "cloud layer" caused by a lifetime of misinformed negative thinking, then and only then will you experience the natural euphoria attendant to being *healthfully* human. Another advantage to this sort of "house cleaning" is that you will free up and gain access to the enormous amount of energy formerly misspent doubting and resisting yourself. This energy will enable you to re-motivate and improve conditions in every area of your life—naturally, confidently, and enthusiastically.

Relax that "arm" and straighten that "leg." Fashion yourself some better fitting "idea wear," why don't you?

-10- | The Michelangelo Method

There is a story about Michelangelo that beautifully typifies the work ahead of you. After the artist presented a wondrous statue of an elephant he had recently finished sculpting out of rock, an admirer approached Michelangelo. "How did you ever create such a magnificent, lifelike beast?" he asked. "It was really quite simple," Michelangelo replied. "I merely removed everything from the stone that was *not* the elephant."

Instead of having to create the elephant, Michelangelo understood that he needed only to uncover it. He believed, and justifiably so, that the elephant was already *in* the stone. You must have the same conviction regarding your inherent splendor and the work of art that already is your life.

Let this, then, be your new creed: **Health/joy/prosperity is my natural state. It already exists within me and is mine to experience *when I release everything that I am not.*** What "you are not"—all your fears, doubts, resistances, angers, guilt, sadness . . . all your issues, even the many doubts you undoubtedly feel about what you have just read here—are *your* "not the elephant" parts. They all are merely temporary misunderstandings—encrusted overlays—concealing your beauty within them.

~~~

Remember, you are a spirit/mind/body continuum of energy, connecting and incorporating your inner world of thought and feeling with your outer world of physical body and material universe. To improve the quality of your life, this system must be clear, free of genetic and societal imprints at the alpha level of who you are (the consciousness/cause of you), so that you may create your "reality" (the omega or effect level) freely and with purpose.

To do this, you will not only need to tap into and renegotiate your body's nonbeneficial "truths" (or what it has historically believed to be true) but you must also learn to listen to its likes and dislikes. In so doing, you will finally level the playing field, making change not only possible, but simple and easy. Your new life will be the natural offspring of an unencumbered free-will and limitless free-choice.

The total access that you will soon gain will yield critical information to you. This information has long been missing from your emotional/spiritual teachings, but nevertheless, it is information that has been "running the show." How would you like to have learned to ride that first bike of yours going uphill? So far, you have suffered an equivalent handicap in your personal growth work—trying to reconcile your desires with your phantom fears and resistances. Please listen and take this next bit to heart: *You cannot become **more** of something that you wholly already **are**. You can only remember, by releasing that which you never were in the first place.*

~~~

Most of us need assistance in reaching, then renegotiating, our non-supportive subconscious thoughts and feelings. We need help distinguishing between the elephant and the stone. Within these pages you will learn how to do this for yourself. You will, in no time at all, have near total access to your innermost tenacious energies—your skewed interpretations and slanted perspectives. Perhaps more importantly, you will also come to recognize your damaging subconscious expectations. As you progress, pay particularly close attention to the automatic "naysayer" within you. Keep an open mind. And above all, be patient with yourself. You come by your fears and skeptical nature honestly. Give yourself time to get used to the ideas expressed, and the methods taught, herein. Remember, too, that personal growth is a process—a process of incremental gain. Just take it a step at a time and before long you will be in a brand new place.

Now, before you can become a modern-day Michelangelo, you will want to examine and understand the nature of the "stone" in which you currently find yourself lodged. That is, your hardened ideas, conditions, and skepticisms.

-11- The Light At the End Of the Tunnel Is *Not* An Oncoming Train

You were, I contend, not born skeptical. More likely, you were convinced or coerced early on to trade in your inherent playfulness, along with a healthy portion of your individuality, for the "privilege" of not being left to the wolves. Well, here you are years down the road, long ago having purged your natural *joie de vivre* and Self-trust—the essential precursors of spontaneity and enthusiasm. In their stead, you planted an other-oriented concern for acceptance in hopes of feeding your need to be loved. You did not wittingly do this. You did not realize at the time that you were trading Manhattan Island for a handful of worthless trinkets. It is no wonder you have become a skeptic.

And it is only now, as you reach for a fuller, more satisfying, more peacefully secure way of life, that you begin to sense a "can't get there from here" quality to your existence . . . to feel that insatiable longing echoing within you. Yes, it is only now that you truly appreciate how disconnected you feel, how badly your personal foundations have been compromised . . . seemingly irreparably so.

~~~

Truth is, deep down, there is much pain, anger, resentment, and fear within most of us. This keeps our focus outward, as we are understandably reluctant to turn our gaze or experience within—toward the discomfort. However, it is *within* where our "truth" must be sought if it is to be found. To move to a higher ground—

and better our conditions—we must first understand that our emotional feelings of a negative, limiting, or painful nature are almost always the result of misguided thought. Consequently, lasting spiritual/personal growth may only be had when we discover, express, and release this thought. Simply put: *Changing the course of your life requires you to change the course of your thinking.* Period.

~~~

Even after years of psychotherapy, many of us are still unable to alter our habitual thinking. We typically wind up in a place where we are vastly better informed, but for all intents and purposes, we are just about as unhappy and as pessimistic as ever.

It is true that tackling our conscious feelings, thoughts, and behaviors "head-on"—analyzing ourselves if you will—proves not entirely futile. The process does, after all, offer up a rationale for the multitude of disparate and disparaging messages with which we relentlessly bombard ourselves. But most of the "ah-ha's" we encounter along the traditional self-help or psychotherapeutic trail do little to shift the fundamentally compromised feelings we *subconsciously* carry, and so we remain stuck, unable to improve the day-to-day, moment-by-moment experience of our lives.

If you are to finally free yourself from the awkward, insecure feelings which you long ago grudgingly assented to as "How it feels to be me" (your Michelangeloic 'rock'), you will need to distinguish yourself from the misguided subconscious beliefs that hold these adverse feelings in place. Only then may you have a first-hand experience of your true, essential, spiritual Self.

Mystic Secret 2: It was the avoidance of painful feelings that inspired you to begin building your emotional armor—getting you into "trouble" in the first place. Now it is the gentle soliciting, the welcoming back of those feelings (backtracking Hansel and Gretel style), that will allow you to re-associate, to re-integrate, and to get yourself out of whatever physical or emotional predicaments into which you may have inadvertently stumbled.

Exercise 2: Drawing on Shakti Gawain's work in the area of visualization (specifically, her classic book *Creative Visualization*, which I recommend to you), take a survey starting with the words *"I'll never get what I want because . . . ."* We are still in the early preparatory stages. Here, "clearing" is the essential process. In this exercise, list as many reasons you can *quickly* come up with—in an "off the top of your head" fashion—why the notion of having the things you want may feel more like a pipe-dream than a reasonable expectation.

For instance: *"I'll never get what I want because . . ."*
—I'm not smart enough.
—No one likes me.
—Women are discriminated against.
—I'm too lazy.
—Life is unfair.
—I don't want to give my mother the satisfaction of having any successful offspring. (Whoa! Now there's a high price to pay for revenge—but many are willing to pay it.)
—I'd feel guilty doing better than Dad did. (An equally high price to pay for loyalty)
—Etc.

Be creative and spontaneous. Let this list be stream of consciousness. You will want to save these statements and put them through The Emotional Detoxx as outlined on pages 95 through 97. In the meantime, do your best to make as complete a list as possible.

-12- | The Troll Who Lived Under the Bridge

P_{ain} . . . I have always had a very low threshold for it—
emotional or otherwise. This did not exactly make me a sissy,
just a miserably anxious kid. Because I could not tolerate my
emotional pain, I was forced to rationalize my way out of it.
Eventually, though, this would mean that somewhere down
the road, I would have to challenge and renegotiate all the
expectation and belief that I had concocted for that purpose.
Therefore, long before The Emotional Detoxx, there was *The
Truth and the Lie Game.*

So much of my thinking had been dedicated to self-doubt and
criticism, that as an early act of self-recovery, I found that I
needed to scrutinize nearly every thought I had. I began sorting
through my beliefs, distinguishing between those that seemed
founded in some "truth" (empirically provable) and those which,
after much examination, appeared to be blatant distortions.

I was so convinced of my own worthlessness that I entertained
virtually no positive thoughts of myself. So one-sided was this,
however, that I began to question the plausibility of it. How
could it be that I had turned out so horribly? I would tell my
therapist that I could walk into a room of a thousand people and
know that I was "less" than any of them. "Less how?" he would
ask. "Less talented, less intelligent, less good looking . . . you
name it, and I would have less of it."

As I was to discover, this decision I made about my worth
was not the result of any rational process. It was a foregone
conclusion. The image I carried of myself was grossly

misshapen. Emotionally I was the equivalent of the troll who lived under the bridge. By living in the concept (thought) of this as opposed to the experience (feeling), I had quieted the pain, but I had also robbed myself of any direct contact with life. My low self-esteem was literally locked in the dungeon created by my damaging self-concepts.

It was clearly in hope of proving myself wrong about me, and freeing my spirit by establishing an unfiltered encounter with life, that I began examining my beliefs. What *was* the truth? Was I really as awful as I imagined? This process became more and more structured, and it evolved into what I later dubbed *The Truth and the Lie Game*—the search for and reclamation of my true "Self."

~~~

I began to question every negative thought I had, and take it from me, that was nearly all my thinking. *The Game* consisted of my finding support for, or opposition to, each belief. Nine times out of ten, my negative feelings and beliefs about my world or myself were unsubstantiated empirically—unprovable in any way.

I was amazed to see how skewed my perceptions were relative to what was currently discernable. My views seemed based in some past "reality," in which now only my emotions still dwelled. Intellectually it made no sense to feel the way that I did, yet emotionally it made no sense to feel otherwise. Given this tug-of-war, though, my emotions *always* won.

In the early days of *The Game*, I would ask my best friends what *they* thought of me, thinking that somehow their objectivity could serve me in some way. But this outward approach proved futile. I was constantly comparing myself to them and always coming up short. My friends found it hard to believe that I could have such low self-esteem. They saw me in a very different light.

I listened to their kind words, but I could never really hear them.
I could not hear them, because I could not *believe* them.

> "Dependent as we are on the nuclear family, on the
> attentions of, at best, two overcommitted parents, and
> oriented as we are to the development of independence,
> our culture tends to foster the internalization of what-
> ever absence was initially present.
> " . . . .There remains in (the) individual a gnawing
> sense of emptiness, a flaw that the person perceives
> as lying within himself or herself, rather than in early
> personal experiences."[1]
> —Mark Epstein, M.D., *Thoughts Without A Thinker*

~~~

My condition seemed permanent. I was somehow painfully and
basically flawed. My childhood perspective was starting to have
a devastating affect on me, but without the tools that I would
later develop, I was at a loss to know what was really going on.
And with all the intellectual tail-chasing that I was doing, I was
not getting any closer to "home" or to any experience of life that
remotely resembled joy or a sense of well-being.

But *The Game* had helped me to see how unreasonable my
beliefs were, and this proved to be an important step on the way
to letting go. I invite you to play and to see what this process
might mean for you.

~~~

For better or worse, my thinking did accomplish one thing. It
kept me in my head, out of the direct line of fire of my painful
feelings. But eventually I would want to feel again (numb and/or

in denial is no way to live). And I would need all the information I could gather and all the courage I could muster before I would choose to brave the sharp side of feelings' double-edged sword, one more time.

Mystic Secret 3: *Joy is nonconditional.* It cannot depend on your landing that job, getting a date with so and so, or meeting someone else's expectations of you. These things can too easily be taken from you. Your joy is too precious to be left in the hands of others. Since happiness is predominantly an inner production—with perspective playing the vital role—your general attitude will, to a great degree, dictate the quality of your life.

Exercise 3: Take your list from Exercise 2 and begin challenging your litany of reasons "why." That is **not** to say that you should deny your feelings. These are quite real to you, I am sure. Real as they may seem, this does not mean they are objectively true. In this exercise, you are beginning to question beliefs about yourself that you have simply taken for granted. This is a habit that you can no longer afford. Much of what you hold in consciousness was impressed upon you. You need to start sorting through your beliefs, because many negative thoughts you have about yourself are the result of someone else's error in judgment. Others arose from unfair comparisons that you made between yourself and another. Neither of these methods can possibly lead you to the truth about, nor joy within, yourself. If a negative belief happens to be empirically provable, you would work on correcting the inner condition that gave rise to it. That, however, is beyond the scope of this particular exercise.

The Truth and the Lie Game: Take one item off your Exercise 2 "Why" list and write it at the top of a clean piece of paper. On the left side of the page, list all the evidence you can find to support this belief, feeling, or contention; and on the right, record an alternate interpretation.

For example: "I'm Lazy"

Your Historical Interpretation	**An Alternate Interpretation**
I watch too much TV.	I love educational TV, old movies, documentaries, and 60 Minutes.
I don't like working.	I hate my job, but give me something I enjoy doing and I'm like a dog with a bone.
I think about women (men) too much.	This is just compensation for my feelings of low self-esteem. Maybe I should improve my self-image.
I just want to have fun.	I think life *should* be fun. I know that flies in the face of my father's/mother's style, but hey, I don't want to end up as unhappy as they seem to be.
I hate responsibility.	I like thinking for myself. And I *don't* like being told what to do. Maybe I just hate being held responsible for what other people think I *should* be doing.
I know I'm lazy 'cause Dad used to yell at me all the time to "do this"or to "do that." He was *always* on my case. I must be a good-for-nothin'. . . he said so.	Dad seemed angry all the time and was probably overwhelmed by all of his responsibilities. Maybe he took his frustration out on *me*. M a y b e . . . I was just being a normal kid.

By making a graphic representation of your interpretations, you can begin to get a sense of their character and tone, and start to appreciate the extent to which they have been ruling you by appearing as if they were the only possible or legitimate ones.

It's an important step to realize that there could be other valid ways of viewing yourself and/or the painful events of your past. In doing so, you can begin to undo the damage done by your historically negative self-perspective. You are after full self-disclosure. Don't be a human ostrich.

-13- | The Mess Is the Message

In your ongoing efforts to release that which you are not—your sabotaging beliefs and resisted emotions—one thing will usually become very clear . . . You do not feel very good about who you are, or I should say, who you *think* you are. The reason? Somewhere along the line, you lost touch with your Actual Self. There is no longer an acceptable sense of "me" to which you enjoy relating, and very little good can come of that. Mark Epstein, M.D., the author of *Thoughts Without a Thinker* and a psychotherapist with a Buddhist perspective, writes, "We do not want to admit our (perceived) lack of substance to ourselves and, instead, strive to project an image of completeness, or self-sufficiency. The paradox is that, to the extent that we succumb to this urge, we are estranged from ourselves and are *not real.*"[2]

The unhappy, unfortunate truth is that most of us were not cared for best when it mattered most. There may not have been any malicious intent, but it doesn't matter—the "damage" was done, nonetheless. Physically you may have grown full-size, though recent studies indicate that sustained childhood stress levels can actually inhibit a person from reaching full height/weight potential. In all probability you were left feeling "half-baked," emotionally stunted—dwarfed by imposition and indoctrination—a shadow of your real self.

On the brighter side, the good news is that you are well equipped to successfully finish the job of raising yourself. In fact, you are in a far better position than your parents or anyone else ever was or could be. Your job is to now set things right, to "turn back the clock," so to speak, to pick up where you emotionally veered off your evolutionary path.

Interestingly, although you will soon be able to release your nonessential energies, discovering who you actually are is a far more slippery proposition. It's a lot like trying to pick up a drop of mercury, really. Why? Because identity is essentially amorphous, so you may forever remain a mystery, even to yourself. This is not a liability, however. It simply speaks to the virtually limitless potential that you are. This noted, a focus on your *experience* of yourself, while relaxing the need for a definition, becomes key. *This shift to "How does it **feel** to be me?"—a fluid and moving perspective—as opposed to "Who am I?"—a static view—could, in and of itself, change your life—yielding both immediate and long-term benefit. For you are a human **being**. You are a verb—not a noun.*

~~~

Sadly, for the moment at least, many people are experiencing themselves as "lost" in some way. If you are, you are a member of a growing society of wayward souls, addicted to escaping what feels like your primordial pain. Drugs, sex, food, alcohol, work, shopping, or TV serve to numb you into what you consider "tolerable" limits. You probably no longer champion yourself. Instead, you are likely to be forever complaining, in hope of rescue. Even many of us who eventually brave our way to the therapist's chair or couch often substitute any genuine desire for self-actualized wellness for the elusive dream of being saved.

You hurt and you do not know why. Or you think you know, but somehow as you sift through the rubble of your fragmented life, the pieces do not quite add up. Then as you struggle to rebuild, you seem to be shy a piece or two; the "holes" in your soul aching with an emptiness as bad or worse than any physical or emotional abuse you ever endured.

If you live with pain, then your first cuts, those earliest emotional woundings, oftentimes pre-memory, have never healed, nor have they left you, as the saying goes, emotionally scarred. If you are in pain, there is no scar. There isn't even a scab. You hurt because your first cuts remain open wounds that continue to "bleed." With every doubt, every bout of depression, every fear, anxiety, and panic attack—with every emotionally related disease, you shed another drop.

I realize this may sound dark, but I mean it to be the very opposite. It is precisely *because* your wounds have not closed, that you have cause for great hope, as pain is your guide through the healing process. It is only when you are in pain that healing can begin, for you will fix only that which you can sense *needs* fixing.

A closed wound, one which you no longer feel, is a *fait accompli*, an accomplished fact—the period at the end of a life's sentence. Pain, therefore, means hope, and hope is the first, most important prerequisite for healing. Of course, there are all kinds of emotional pain, ranging from severe depression and acute anxiety, to a relatively benign nagging feeling that you are procrastinating again. The intensity is not the issue. The message is in the discomfort. The mess is the message.

~~~

If you are in pain, then you are in luck. And you say, "Thanks, I'd like to be a little less lucky." But if this really were so, you would expect that the more pain you were in, the more hope there would be of a healing. This is indeed borne out in my years of practice. Pain is the great motivator. Have you ever known anyone to want to change themselves or their situation when they were comfortable? If you find yourself saying, "Why should I bother, things will never be any different anyway," then you simply are not in sufficient enough pain so as to seek relief.

Relief, you see, especially in the early stages of self-evolution, is the first, best reason to bother. If you are not seeking relief in earnest, you simply have not reached a point of critical mass *vis-à-vis* your pain.

~~~

But as much as pain might now strangely be considered your ally, it was the primary reason that you got off-track in the first place. As a little person, the littlest things hurt greatly. So you— like me— devised a brilliant "solution." You ran to the shelter of your analytical mind. Here, you discovered that you could ease your emotional pain by repressing it. The problem with this was that, in so doing, you undoubtedly created either a psychosomatic disease or a covert or overt compensatory style—such as aggressiveness or timidity. Or you could have rationalized your emotions, placing blame on others or yourself. In that way, so long as you were thinking, you found that you did a lot less feeling. Neat trick.

The only problem with this way of dealing (or not dealing) with your pain, was that you inadvertently "jammed" your ability to feel anything good as well. Having fled to the "safety" of your mind, you now typically live in thought, not in a direct, connected experience of each moment. This analytical approach to life can lead to a sense of separation, then to isolation, and finally to despair and mental and/or physical breakdown.

Purposeful living, with Joy as a primary goal, requires that you return to a direct encounter with the Now. In essence, on a feeling level, you as a child learned to "forget" the present in an effort to relieve your pain. Remembering to remember it becomes one of your most important new chores.

~~~

Thinking and feeling do not mix. Like oil and water, they pretty much stay out of each other's way. In terms of recovery, this will mean that you will need to "let go" your mind's grip on life. You will need to stop filtering every experience through judgment and analysis and risk the return of *all* feeling—both the pleasant and the not-so-pleasant. If you are to step into heaven, you must be willing to brave the possibility of hell. Learning that the big "ouches" of childhood can now be handled is the adult equivalent of challenging the closet door boogey man. All demons are the same. They are vapor. They are inventions.

As self-evident as all this may sound, it takes courage and creativity to take this information from the realm of the theoretical into the practical.

-14- | My Red Letter Day

About fifteen years ago, I had finally had enough. I had, at last, reached the point where I could no longer bear at least one aspect of my mutilated self-image—my life-long asthma. So, one night while meditating, I proposed a deal with God. I told Him that I would never again doubt His existence (something I was historically prone to do), if I could get rid of my asthma. I can recall thinking that this was pretty presumptuous of me— expecting God to work a miracle on my behalf (that is, if He existed at all). But I was at my wit's end and desperate to be rid of this chronic respiratory nightmare, once and for all.

Weeks passed . . . and no answer. Then, one day, I ran into an old friend who I hadn't seen in over a year. Carla was still the attractive, vibrant woman I remembered her to be. Yet as I listened to her speak and watched her animated form, I became aware of an incredible, yet inexplicable change in her. At a break in the catching up, I asked if anything had happened that would account for what I was sensing.

Carla enthused that six months earlier she had not been feeling very well and so had decided to see a "healer." This person discovered a long-standing, low-grade infection in her system—telling Carla that she had had this condition since her early teens. The healer then prescribed a simple homeopathic remedy for its cure.

"Within a month," Carla crescendoed, "I felt better than I ever had!"

Well, I may not literally be from Missouri, but I might as well be. This was plenty to swallow. Yet I could see with my own eyes that something remarkable had taken place in my friend's life. So I asked for the healer's name and phone number. The air of mystery and magic was just too much to ignore. Besides, maybe this chance meeting had something to do with my prayer/deal with God, now nearly two months old. I called the phone number, making an appointment for the following week.

~~~

I entered Stephanie Ewings' house on a cool, crisp autumn morning. While not knowing exactly what to expect, I felt slightly taken aback when a pretty woman in her late twenties introduced herself to me. She had the disposition of a carefree elf, laughing loudly and often.

Stephanie led me into her ranch-style home, down a long hallway, and into a second-bedroom-turned-office. There was no examining table, just a couple of chairs, and the walls were lined with tall wooden cabinets. These cabinets were filled with what appeared to be thousands of little brown glass vials. The vials, in turn, contained legions of tiny white spherical "pills."

After explaining that these were homeopathic, a word I had heard but had little use for, Stephanie asked me the purpose of my visit. Timidly I replied, "I'd like to get rid of my asthma."

She laughed a wonderfully loud belly laugh, then began to look at me very seriously for a few seconds, as if somehow sizing me up. "Alright," she announced, "we can do that." Her certainty quickly became my disbelief. "Oh really," I mocked, "how can you be so sure?" After all, I had endured eight years of allergy shots to no avail, still suffering from chronic life-long asthma nearly everyday. Stephanie gently turned to me and, with a "Glinda-the-Good-Witch-of-the-North" enchanted sort of smile, said ever so matter-of-factly, *"Because you are ready to give it up."*

This enigmatic young woman then began her "examination." She asked me to hold one arm out at a ninety-degree angle from my body, and began what she would later call "muscle testing." With one hand, she applied downward pressure to my outstretched arm, asking me to resist her with "equal force" while she positioned her other hand systematically over various parts of my head and torso. Mumbling something about meridian lines and imbalances, she entered her findings on a yellow legal-sized notepad, scribbling wildly.

Within ten minutes, she was finished with this portion of the show and rose to remove a single bottle of pills from one of her cabinets. Putting the tiny glass vial in my hand and my hand on my abdomen, she briefly re-tested. Then, giving an affirmative sort of grunt, she spoke, "In addition to this, I want you to pick up some Bach Flower Remedies. They'll treat the asthma from the vantagepoint of your personality."

Whoa! What the heck was she *talking* about?

To say that I was in a daze when I left Stephanie's house that day would be putting it way too mildly. Dazed and confused for sure, and certain really of only one thing: This had to be the most bizarre approach to healing I had ever encountered. I was totally unconvinced of its merits and doubly doubtful of any favorable results.

But then I remembered my deal with God, my friend's story, and the transformation I had witnessed in her that had spirited me to Stephanie in the first place. I decided to go to the homeopathic pharmacy, buy the remedies, and begin the simple two-week regime.

~~~

Because late autumn usually signaled the end of my asthma "season," I was unsure of the effectiveness of Stephanie's program until mid-winter. At that time I traveled to Chicago to visit some old friends—friends who owned both a cat and a dog. I slept soundly the first night in their home, oddly not even thinking about the animals or the fact that under "normal" conditions I would be wheezing my head off by now, unable to sleep without medication. The next night proved the same, and by the following morning, it finally dawned on me what was going on. I went over to the animals and began to pet and play with them. To my utter amazement, I did not wheeze, sneeze, itch, or twitch one single bit!

I was filled with joy; I mean real euphoria. I thanked God. Then I thanked Stephanie. Then I cried.

~~~

I must have been in a mild state of shock. Or maybe a life-long veil had suddenly been lifted from my eyes, because the world now seemed very bright, filled with all sorts of new possibilities. Not only was the absence of asthma incredible, but so was my newly established faith—no, not faith—*knowledge*. A universal intelligence, "God" if you will, had actually responded to me. My concept of God was no clearer now than it had been before my "miracle," but that did not matter. Some Intelligent Energy, some "Causal Force" had colluded with me on my behalf. If I could do this, if I could get rid of my asthma, I could do anything. My life would never be the same. No longer would there or could there be a delineation between "reality" and "spirituality." I now *knew* they were one-and-the-same.

I knew something else, too. Change *was* possible. But the mystery of life, it now seemed to me, was even more mysterious than ever.

-15- Searching for Bigfoot: Imprints in The Emotional Sand

I decided to learn as much as I could about how this type of transformation was possible. I had long been preparing for a career in the emotional healing arts, spending years studying alternative methods of change. But seven years of psychotherapy, eight years of psychoanalysis and psychoanalytic training, a ministerial Ph.D. in Metaphysics, and dozens of seminars and certification programs had not prepared me for the shift that I had just experienced. I needed to know more.

Stephanie Ewings was gracious enough to work with me, generously sharing her remarkable methods. Her ideas and techniques complemented my own emerging philosophy and growing conviction that the psyche, the body, and the world were somehow all woven together into a universal "fabric." I learned how to muscle test myself, something you too will soon learn. This proved to be a powerful, relentlessly accurate tool for accessing what had previously been unreachable, undetectable information—what I began to call "body belief." I knew that if I were to ever really be happy and exercise my full potential, I would need to uncover and finally deal with these mysterious and elusive energies.

Accessing and addressing hidden thought, coupled with the other forms of esoteric metaphysical work that I had been doing, proved to be the one-two punch I needed to change my unwanted psychological, emotional, physical, and even spiritual conditions. What appeared to be happening was, through Kinesiological (muscle) testing, I was going much deeper, much faster. As a result, I was able to heal my oldest disharmonic energies, those frozen-in-time thought-forms that had been stored deep in my body on a cellular level. I was racing through evolutionary work that would have taken years just to uncover via traditional psychotherapeutic means. How was this possible?

Here's how . . . Remember, you are a continuum of energy. On one end is your mind and spirit, and on the other is your body and the physical world. The latter is the expression in physical form of who you are "within"—mentally and spiritually. Physical experience, therefore, becomes key to understanding the sponsoring energies creating it. If you want to improve your life, you need to pay particular attention to, and renegotiate, the disharmonious information that got stuck in your physical body so long ago. This information has energetically rippled out ever since, and it has been made manifest as your fears, diseases, and undesirable conditions. Successful Thought Farming depends on your continued diligence and an artful awareness of yourself at your deepest levels. Let's look at the mechanics of this more closely, shall we?

~ ~ ~

Thought Farming—creation via intention—works inside out and upside-down. Well, it doesn't actually work upside-down, but it appears to, due to the limits of our knowledge and the restrictions of our sensory equipment. Much in the way that our eyes see an inverted image that is then righted in the brain, Thought Farming requires that we mentally turn things around as well. Only this time, we have to do it consciously and deliberately. Do not get discouraged. It's really a very natural process.

What all this means is that if we are to manifest new relationships with ourselves, our lovers, our parents, or our world, we need to establish a *working* appreciation of this fact: **Before any life experience, there exists a sponsoring belief.**

This is quite literally true of *any* experience. Initially, this might sound counter-intuitive. Why, for instance, would anyone form a belief about something *before* they had an experientially based reason to do so?

Well, they wouldn't. Assuredly, some parental or societal "bruising" is at work and ought to be examined and healed. This is the typical grist for the talk-therapy mill. But "experience" comes in all shapes and sizes. Our interest here will be in *all* the ways, actual and virtual, in which our essential selves (our non-belief-based selves) have been compromised, "stepped-on," squashed Bigfoot-style by our adopted "body belief."

~~~

Here is where we part with tradition . . . There is trauma that can be *inherited*, disharmonic belief-energy that I have begun to call "negative virtual-experience." The cells of our bodies store emotional impressions, in addition to other genetic material, along the DNA strand. These imprints are of varying energetic frequency, each resisted emotion leaving its own "footprint." Once having become genetically available, they are passed on both intercellularly (during cellular regeneration), and generationally (through procreation).

You want proof? Of course you do. I needed it, too. And when I finally found it, I knew I had discovered the missing piece of the therapy puzzle. I knew, too, that I would one day leave my therapist's office for the last time, and that I would help others to do the same. Now it's your turn.

~~~

Every seven years, your body recreates and renews itself. Why aren't you given a clean slate with each incarnation? Because every new cell accepts the blueprint of an outgoing one. This is an extraordinary, mystical process; and, for the most part, we can be extremely grateful for the way in which it keeps us, us. But self-reproduction has its drawbacks. For instance, if you tend to be timid, or for that matter diabetic, your old dying cells will transmit this tendency, this "idea," to the brand new ones. Why? Because this is who they energetically "think" they are.

One client, a rather gifted writer, describes the process as reminiscent of the storytelling that once took place around Native American Indian campfires. The old and dying chief turns to his young son, filling him with the "wisdom" of his years (prejudice and all); the wide-eyed youth absorbs every nuance as the campfire burns down to its final flickering embers, and then . . . the Chief is dead. A pretty good analogy really. Except our cells "listen" *much* more closely than did the young brave, emulating their "fathers" far more faithfully.

The cell's DNA codifies with digital accuracy an overall reflection of its physical and emotional state—something called "tagged" energy. The truth of this is not only tacitly obvious in all our lives, but provable through muscle testing. Consequently, not only is your hair color, eye color, height, and general physical body size and type inherited and regenerated, but also your predisposition to certain illness, as well as any cellular "story" of past trauma severe enough so as to have left an energetic imprint on the DNA. This is precisely why it is so frustratingly difficult to simply try and talk ourselves off our emotional roller coasters. These energies are quite literally ingrained.

~~~

Time and again, using muscle testing, I have uncovered belief systems and energy patterns in clients and myself where the origin tested not only prior to birth, but also *prior to conception*. Initially, I was sure that I was coming up with a false reading. But as I tested further, client after client revealed a preconceptive predisposition to countless emotional and personality related genetic tendencies. How is this possible?

Remember, much in the same way that cells follow the DNA code in regenerating body tissue, they pass along this genetic information in procreation.

Long before your birth, your ancestors were busy accumulating centuries of life experience. Most of this was simple, nontoxic, everyday fare. Some, on the other hand, proved traumatic, with consequences that energetically reached deep into their cellular make-up—their body-unconscious. Once at this level, an energetic imprint was formed. And because it now had modified the DNA itself, it was regenerated—not only within this early ancestor, but transmitted genetically to their offspring. If these imbalances were not corrected sometime during the preconceptive stage of that new life, the tendencies would again be passed on to their offspring. And so on, and so on. . . right down to you.

What I found was that just because the sperm had not yet become acquainted with the egg, creating the zygote, evolving into the organism eventually to be called "you," it does not mean that your genes did not exist. It only means that the exact combination of those genes had yet to be decided.

~~~

Many second and third generation sons and daughters of holocaust survivors test "positive," as if *they themselves* had endured the concentration camp atrocities. That material was genetically available at the time of their conception. The energetic weight of ancestral trauma and the subsequent imprinting and genetic transference appeared to account for the strong feelings of identification experienced among members of persecuted ethnic groups. Jews, Armenians, Catholics, and Blacks—all represented within my clientele—offer chilling witness to this phenomenon.

M. had incredibly strong *resisted* feelings of anger and persecution; this was despite the fact that he had had a relatively benign upbringing, racially speaking. It took several sessions of "peeling the onion" before we got down to an identity M. carried originating with his Civil Wartime grandmother. So brutally treated in slavery was she, that after years of abuse, she was eventually hung. Discovering and releasing the cause of his profound feelings of persecution allowed M. to feel, for the first time in his life, that he was finally "free." His inherited resentment and rage, once tapped, melted into tears, and drained in torrents from his body.

Following this dramatic pivotal session, M.'s "luck" immediately began to change. He started booking a series of national television commercials, which he still routinely gets, and has gone on to become a happy, working, Thought Farming actor.

~~~

T. demonstrated a remarkable similarity in lifestyle to her biological father . . . who she had never met. T.'s mother had revealed to her that T.'s father was a Catholic missionary, torn between a vow of celibacy and his love for T. and her mother. After much personal torment, he finally decided to leave the family and continue his missionary work in Africa.

Now in her late twenties, T. feels the need to help her fellow humans in ways that far exceed a typical good-neighbor policy. She is even driven to help strangers at great personal sacrifice. Additionally, her sexuality, like that of her father's, is a source of considerable pain and confusion. T. leads an active lesbian lifestyle, while professing concern over her inability to share physical intimacy with men, who she also finds attractive. Both her call-to-serve and her frustrating sexual approach/avoidance are direct energetic links to a father she "knows" only by virtue of her genetic inheritance and a handful of stories she has been told.

~~~

P. was extremely shy—as far back as she could remember—especially when it came to her dealings with men. After some preliminary discovery work, P. revealed that her great-grandfather had raped her mother. When I tested, it became clear to both of us that P. carried the trauma of this horror in her own body, passed down genetically (again, easily discernable through muscle testing). Over the years, it had been additionally reinforced, through her mother's perpetual subconscious non-verbal messaging.

The Emotional Detoxx, with its ability to access, address, and renegotiate inherited body-belief, allows for the exploration and the working through of this mysteriously obscure, yet vitally pertinent material.

-16-   Nurture's Nature
         When It Doesn't

Negative imprints through socialization hail from a different neck of the emotional woods than the genetically based. The sequence of a socialized imprint typically starts with someone else's non-supportive opinion or ill treatment of us. This energetically "morphs" into a negative belief about ourselves. If entertained long enough, this belief settles deeper within us as a feeling. Over time, this feeling generalizes into an attitude or physical condition. Left unchecked, attitudes and physical conditions globalize, becoming our life circumstances.

Let's take a look at how this works. Some "other"—typically a parent or close authority figure—presents you with their "negative" energy regularly and with sufficient intensity so that you begin to form a destructive, self-sabotaging belief. This happens because you are more apt to assume the blame for all things "wrong," due to your near total dependency on such persons for survival. Then, too, many beliefs are adopted from our caretakers long before we have the cognitive abilities or the personal experiences from which to formulate our own.

If these second-hand idea/assumptions remain unchallenged, they typically grow into feelings of unworthiness, eventually becoming pervasive attitudes, such as despair, or body conditions, such as asthma or ulcers. Finally, at its greatest impact, this unholy sequence leads to a life circumstance, such as poverty, mental illness, or an "incurable" disease. To the degree to which these energies are nonsupportive—leading us to thought and behavior that inhibit our natural selves—they could and probably would, result, at the very least, in personality disorder and various habitual patterns of self-sabotage. These might range anywhere from overeating to sexual addiction, from nail-biting to suicide.

~~~

Now if Mom or Dad had been more psychologically hip when reprimanding us, they might have known enough to say something like, "What you *did* was bad, and it makes me angry when you *do* things like that," instead of "*You* are bad." Alas, most moms and dads ride roughshod all over us, not realizing the tremendous negative effect they are having on our fragile senses of self-respect. We "buy" their negative messages more easily because they seem more "real" to us, reminiscent, as they are, of our earliest inner conditioning—our feelings of helplessness, and our fears of abandonment and loss. The occasional loving remark or gesture will do little to rebalance the inner scales upon which we measure ourselves. We tilt to the left or to the right, always aware that something is off, bad, or wrong. And we incorrectly assume that that something is us.

~~~

What are these negative imprints? What are they made of (be they societal or genetic), and why are they so tenacious? Well, as you might suspect, like everything else in the universe, they are energy. But these are disharmonic energies that are held deep in the body. They are stored in a state akin to a hologram, at the cellular level, and are formed when emotions are unexpressed.

Hologram-like, these imprints contain the *entire* originally resisted emotional "episode," encoded energetically. This charge is then stored in the body and, if left unchecked, establishes itself—creating a new status quo—rendering the now "accepted" imbalance imperceptible. This phenomenon operates similarly to the coping mechanisms that "vanish" the watch on your wrist. If you were continually aware of all stimuli within and around you, you would be rendered dysfunctional—neuronally overloaded.

So you "numb out" to what you have considered the various *non-life-threatening* stimuli, leaving room on your neuronal pathways for what you naturally assumed were the more important life-sustaining messages. The problem with this way of operating is that you forget that the original distressed condition still lives within you, creating its own brand of truth that goes undetected and unchallenged by your ever-evolving conscious mind. The fact that you do not feel the watch on your wrist does not mean that it is not there. **Hence, a fifty-year-old man can feel just as intimidated by his father today as he did forty-five years ago, and not have a clue as to why.**

~~~

This modus operandi becomes more understandable when we consider what "life-threatening" and "life-sustaining" might have meant to the five-year-old. Any action that seemed to displease the father and incur his anger would have been perceived as life-threatening, due to the near total helpless dependency of the young boy. At this developmental stage, emotional resistance would have probably been considered the most life-sustaining choice, in that it would have prevented the child from having any expression, albeit natural and authentic, that could have inadvertently led to a painful moment of disapproval or rejection, or even physical harm.

If the boy continually chooses this emotional contraction, then, over time, it becomes his new status quo, and he virtually loses all conscious contact with his whole self. Eventually the fifty-year-old will find himself literally "at a loss." He does not understand why he feels the way he does, nor does he know what he can do about it. To him, it seems as though he has always been "this way," feeling as though there were a part of him missing. By virtue of this suspicion alone, there is little hope of his ever believing that he could become something that he feels essentially he is not . . . namely, "whole."

This is the "Catch 22" wherein the successful Thought Farmer *must* ultimately prevail. A first-hand appreciation of the fact that he is neither his thoughts nor his feelings will help him to ignore the seemingly justifiable conclusion that he has reached . . . specifically, that his situation is "impossible."

~ ~ ~

Ram Dass, a.k.a. Richard Alpert, Ph.D., is a man who has contributed greatly to the integration of Eastern spiritual philosophy into Western thought. He has said, "It is possible to liberate awareness from identification with thought, and thus be impeccable in life."[3] This challenge requires considerable discipline and a good helping of trust. It should be noted, however, that success here is *the* pivotal moment in the life of every Thought Farmer— creating probably the most profound, most beneficial personal shift possible.

Perhaps not essentially, but for all intents and purposes, when you succeed here—when you have distinguished yourself from your thoughts and feelings—you are indeed "born again."

Problems cannot be solved
At the same level of awareness
That created them.

Albert Einstein

-17- | Memory Like an Elephant, Stubborn As a Mule

At this point, you might be thinking to yourself, "This is all very well and good in theory, and it seems like the approach might even actually work for some people, but I can't just choose new beliefs, feelings, or behaviors—it's not that easy." Well, don't feel like the Lone Ranger. What you are experiencing is a universal "thorn" that has been in the side of mankind possibly forever, and is probably the biggest mixed-blessing we have in being human. Believe it or not, this arch-nemesis, this spoiler of an easy evolution . . . is our memory.

Now, memory is undeniably essential for growth and the exercise of individual will. Remembering what choices we have made in the past, and the resulting experience, is crucial to our living life purposefully. Life without memory would be chaotic, terrifying, and perhaps even impossible.

> "The Greeks personified memory as lady Mnemosyne. Mother of the nine muses, she was believed to have given birth to all the arts and sciences. It is valid to consider memory the oldest mental skill, from which all others derive, for, if we weren't able to remember, we couldn't follow the rules that make other mental operations possible."[4]

As far reaching in importance as it is, the best use for memory that I ever came across was the one offered in *The Nature of Personal Reality*. Here, Jane Roberts, a channeler speaking for the spirit "Seth," introduced a concept called "natural guilt." This is not the Jewish or Catholic variety of guilt with which so many of us are all too familiar. Natural guilt, according to Seth, occurs as the recollection of a similar past event is triggered through association. If the memory is pleasant, natural guilt would suggest that we repeat our previous response in some fashion. If unpleasant, it would ask that we choose a new response. This seems so simple. Then why don't we just do it?

Well, there is a dark, almost monstrous side to memory. Although it is ostensibly an impartial fact retrieval system, *memory seems to consciously favor pleasant recollections, while subconsciously "favoring" unpleasant or painful ones.* I am not nearly as concerned with the coping mechanisms that allow for more positive conscious recall, since these are generally not as problematic. My immediate concern is with what the mind seems to stubbornly cling to in the subconscious.

~ ~ ~

In the movie *Pretty Woman*, Julia Roberts plays call-girl-cum-Cinderella to Richard Gere's princely white knight. At one point, as she struggles to accept a compliment he has just given her, she says, "The bad stuff is easier to believe—ever notice that?" She is unable to see herself in the same heavenly light in which Gere's character has begun to view her.

Fact is, they can both far more easily recognize the good in each other, than they can in themselves. More importantly, they are willing to *believe* what they see. This means much to them, and each becomes a catalyst for growth for the other. Why is it that we seem to need other people's help before we can begin to see ourselves in a more positive light?

The reason for this goes back to early, probably prehistoric childhood, of which we have little or no conscious memory, but deadly subconscious recall. Here, in union with Mother, we feel principally what is mirrored back to us—we, the *secondary* light. We are either the reflected "glow" or the dark-side, eclipsed moon to our mother's source "sun." Our sense of ourselves comes from relation to, and reflection off, this critical "other." This early dependence on the outside world—the "other" vis-à-vis both our sense of ourselves and our sense of that world—will have to be recognized, understood, and renegotiated before any true autonomy may be had.

The "double-whammy" related to the above unfortunate modus operandi comes in the right/wrong–good/bad judgmental aspect associated with it. Remember, what passed for "wrong," doing something "bad," was anything that displeased our parents. By withholding love at a time like this, the parent inadvertently sends the message, *"You* are bad. And because you are bad, I don't love you anymore. *You* are unlovable." This is intolerable to us. We must find a way to prevent this from ever happening again. But, of course, we can't and it does, and again we get the short end of a cold shoulder. Each time this happens, we feel more and more threatened, more and more convinced of our own worthlessness, and more and more needy of outside approval. This becomes a dynamic for life, after, of course, we have buried most of our originally intolerable pain (along with our memory of it), employing the coping mechanism known as repression.

The *"triple*-whammy" associated with this dependency lies with the overwhelming feeling of helplessness with which we are all born. We view our providers, usually our parents, as *all* good and *all* powerful, since we are completely at their mercy and believe we must think this way for our own sanity/safety. We couldn't possibly fend for ourselves, we contend, and so these "benevolent gods" *better* be right or we are in big trouble. This is the start of our tendency to give others the benefit of the doubt, soaking up what we assume to be their wisdom, attributing unsubstantiated, unearned value to them. Meanwhile we pale miserably by comparison and learn to believe less and less in ourselves. These tendencies must be understood and relinquished.

You take a huge step toward emotional maturity and a healthy control of your life when you begin to give **yourself** *the benefit and everyone else, the doubt.*

The "*quadruple*-whammy" (does it ever end?) surrounding our dependency issue lies in the notion of "deservedness." Because we come from such precarious beginnings and enter a world of punishment and reward, we are tempted to falsely believe that our personal value is contingent upon outside acknowledgment. But even more troublesome is the temptation to think that once recognition is bestowed, that we are now somehow transformed, magically more deserving of what we want. Shades of the Scarecrow's diploma, the Tin Man's heart, and the Lion's medal.

~~~

Contrary to this way of thinking, ongoing deserving is nowhere guaranteed. There is no inherent deserving in one and not in another, either by virtue of early recognition or otherwise. As Tracey Woodward—shaman, analytical consultant, and early mentor of mine—likes to point out: Deserving occurs *after* the fact.

This means that we must first firmly believe in the "haveability" of a goal and the wherewithal to achieve it, then follow through in action, and do the things necessary so as to attain that which we claim to desire. And if we then do indeed succeed in our efforts—it is then and *only* then, that we truly realize what we "deserved." Accordingly, we each deserve exactly what we get. But contrary to popular misconception, this is a *post-* and not a pre-condition.

Shedding the notion of "deservedness" or "non-deservedness" becomes an important step toward self-acceptance and personal and professional success and happiness. Many of you feel as though you were *born* undeserving, and consequently believe that there is no hope of ever feeling otherwise, or of getting the things you say you would like to have. Remember, though, this "hat-in-hand" posture is merely the by-product of your old thinking, and that it is the thinking itself that has made it so.

So, here's the good news, campers: No one has ever been born "undeserving"—or deserving, for that matter. There is no such animal. If you just remember that deserving occurs *after* the fact, and not before, you will be cutting yourself some major, major slack. Remember, when you reach the end of your rope *vis-à-vis* "non-deservedness" or any other belief, something else just might be true. Try letting it go . . . See what happens.

-18- | The Emotional Detoxx Is Born

In the story "The Invisible Man," we find a curious correlate to the challenge before us. In order to be seen, the Invisible Man wraps himself in bandages from head to toe, and when he wishes to disappear, he removes them. In other words, he covers himself up so as to become visible. If you can allow yourself a fresh perspective on your life, you may well find that you have employed a similar technique.

You came into this world as pure awareness. You did not identify yourself with anything or as anyone at all. There was no self-consciousness; you were invisible to yourself. "Whose hands are these?" you might have asked, lying in your crib; or more probably, "What are these strange, flying, fleshy, fingered things?" There was not a "me" that you had yet constructed, having a body, or for that matter, habitual thought, fear, hope, or any of the other accoutrements of what we consider personhood.

"Yet," you said, "people keep picking 'me' up, feeding 'me,' burping 'me,' changing 'me.' What do they see that I do not? There must be a 'me' here, something identifiable, distinguishable. Ah," you continued, "these arms and legs; this pain in my belly when I get hungry; this discomfort when I need changing; this sleepy feeling when I need to rest . . . these things must be 'me.'"

You lost sight of the truth all too soon. You started to feel that you were this "self-conscious thing." You covered yourself with the "soothing, knowing" bandages of thoughts and feelings, with identification with your body and your conditions. You did this for two distinct reasons. First, because thinking eases feeling—

the painful feelings of corporeal life—and second, so that you might "know" yourself as others seem so able to know you; to distinguish you as you; to become visible to yourself. You forgot that you were not any of these things at all, but more magically, *the awareness and the intention behind them.*

You looked at your hands and you said, "These are my hands," as opposed to remembering, "Ah yes, here are those things I've heard called hands that I find so many uses for." You said, "I am self-conscious" as opposed to knowing, "I am the awareness that is feeling self-conscious." You, like the Invisible Man, have covered yourself so as to see yourself, and in the process you have lost sight of Who and What you actually are. Now, if you are so inclined, your job is to make yourself invisible once again, so that you might have an *experience* of Who and What you really are . . . purely, authentically, and intimately.

Releasing attachment to thought, to feeling, and to desire—to the things we normally attribute to "beingness"—has traditionally been seen as the path to enlightenment. I agree. But modern man needs modern tools. With evolution comes new ways of achieving old goals. The Emotional Detoxx is your unwrapping tool. Do not be afraid, for you are letting go of all that you are not . . . and a big piece of that just happens to be your fear.

~ ~ ~

All healing—emotional, physical, and spiritual—begins with a return to an unimpeded flow, the essential "I Am"—your equivalent of Michelangelo's elephant. The Emotional Detoxx (**D**isowning **E**very **T**hought **O**ut to Double-cross (**XX**) you) is designed to help you locate and free up your nonessential (non-elephant) energies. It is, without a doubt, the fast track to a better life. As a good tractor is essential for the farmer to effectively do his work, The Emotional Detoxx is the best friend a Thought Farmer could ever hope to have. I will keep the technical talk to a minimum, but I believe some explanation of the "machinery" is warranted.

Accessing, through muscle testing, your "Michelangeloic stone"—the hardened beliefs that keep you from experiencing your beauty, your true Self as Spirit—is your most powerful weapon against self-deception. Here, where The Emotional Detoxx shines the brightest, conventional psychotherapy and traditional Western-style medicine typically break down or find impasse.

The Emotional Detoxx works by testing the integrity of the body's musculature in the face of various stimuli (don't glaze over, the scientific stuff won't last too long). Those stimuli can be substances such as foods, drugs, fabric, etc., or they can be in the more subtle energetic forms of thoughts, beliefs, and feelings. By introducing a stimulus (food—drug—fabric—belief) into our energy field, we can determine whether that stimulus is disruptive when and if it impedes the normal functioning of our subtle neuro-electrical complex. This can readily be revealed through muscle testing, in that an alteration in the state of this finely tuned network will have immediate impact on our musculature—i.e., a sudden disruption of the neuro-electrical system will briefly diminish any muscle's strength.

Stay with me, I promise not to get unnecessarily technical. Also, I swear to you that there is no hocus-pocus here. Soon you won't have to take my word for any of this. Nor will you need to rely on anecdotal evidence, as your first-hand experience will likely convince you.

~~~

The efficacy of muscle testing, the essence of The Emotional Detoxx, has been established using various mechanical and electrical devices. These include the *Kinesiometer*—which measures the fluctuation of electrical impulses within muscle tissue, the way EKG, ECG, and polygraph tests do—and the *Cybex Dynamometer*—which records variances in muscle strength. These machines measure the actual energetic variation within muscles, and their results testify to the accuracy of muscle testing, supporting its use as a powerful adjunctive tool.

Through an ability or inability to retain muscle strength, a vast array of information can be gathered about us. By using The Emotional Detoxx, you can discover hidden emotional resistance and determine which resisted emotion, when expressed, will return integrity back to the musculature and authenticity and flow back into your life. Here is where The Emotional Detoxx proves indispensable as an evolutionary tool. The end result of this amazing process is the body's renewed ability to heal itself. Couple the "lift" you will experience from releasing resisted emotion and the freedom you will gain from consciously neutralizing that emotion's attendant belief system, and you have some powerful reasons for using The Emotional Detoxx in your ongoing efforts to weed your consciousness garden.

~~~

Essentially, here are the ABCs of what you are about to learn: "When a muscle responds to testing with normal strength, it has proper nerve stimulation. When a muscle responds to testing with below normal strength, there is interference with the normal functioning of the nervous system. We know that specific organs are linked with (our) muscles through the complex pathways and neuronal pools of the central nervous system."[5]

By using this testing device, you can easily determine which of your beliefs interfere with your essential expression of yourself. Once the "ground" of the body unconscious has been cleared of nonbeneficial thought/feeling energy—healthier energy systems can be planted in their place. Without the old toxic resistances to "spoil the soil," the new beliefs and feelings can take root.

The journey to authentic power requires that you
Become conscious of all that you feel . . .
In other words, the optimal path of your soul is the
Choice of awareness, the vertical path.

Gary Zukav—*The Seat of the Soul*

-19- See Me, Feel Me, Touch Me, Heal Me— Learning to Self-Test

The Emotional Detoxx, which uses an "O" ring (thumb to pinky) technique, is as fun and easy to learn as it is powerfully illuminating. The following is a description of hand and finger placement for a right-handed person. If you are left-handed, simply substitute right for left, and vice versa.

The "O" Ring Fingers—With your left hand palm up, touch the tip of your left thumb to the tip of your left little finger (not your index finger). The "O" Ring Fingers can be positioned either tip to tip or finger pad to finger pad.

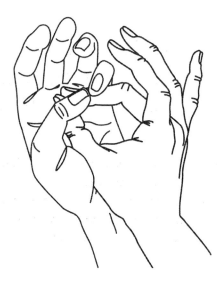

The Test Fingers—To test the integrity of the "O" ring finger muscles, join the thumb and middle finger of your right hand and place it just inside the circle you have created with your left hand. The thumb/little finger of your left hand should be resting on top of the thumb/middle finger of your right.

With the test fingers just inside and beneath the "O" ring fingers, apply outward pressure with the test fingers against the "O" ring fingers. The test finger thumb should be pushing against the inside of the "O" ring finger thumb, the middle finger, pushing against the inside of the "O" ring little (pinky) finger.

~~~

It would serve the accuracy and effectiveness of your testing if you routinely allow yourself a few minutes to relax before beginning. You are looking for a calm inner posture. Under this "neutral" condition, you will not be able to separate the "O" ring fingers with the test fingers. This—and the fact that they are so "handy"—are the reasons we use these muscles for our testing.

Practice applying outward pressure against the inside of the circle created by your "O" ring fingers. Get a feel for the power of the closed "O" ring finger muscles. Understand that you need only gently touch them together. You will not need to pinch them together. Even so, typically, no matter how hard you try, you will still be unable to split the "O" ring fingers apart.

~~~

Now, introduce a statement to the process—something simple— like your first name. State, "My name is (your name)," then try to separate your "O" ring fingers with your test fingers. Use your first name only to begin. If you are aligned with your name, meaning if it carries no negative associative weight for you, you should still be unable to separate your "O" ring fingers. Many people with whom I work do not like their names, and their "O" ring fingers actually go weak when testing this. In these cases, we need to clear the negative charge they have on their names. Names are very important, as they are our most often used personal labels. If you are not strengthened by, or at the very least neutral about your name, identifying yourself with a name that irritates you will weaken you. This can have a disastrous effect on your life.

Next, state where you live—"I live at (your address)"—and once again try to separate your "O" ring fingers using the lateral outward pressure of your test fingers. Again, you should be unable to separate them. *Remember that you will always want to apply **equal force** after each statement, both with the "O" ring fingers in attempting to keep them together and with the test fingers in your efforts to split the "O" ring fingers apart.* If you do not use equal force, you will have no point of reference for your testing. With a little practice, you will get a feel for this.

Now, introduce something you know to be untrue. If you are a blond, you could say, "I have dark brown hair," and test that. In this case, using the *same* pressure with the test fingers, you should be able to separate the "O" ring fingers. Different people are able to create different amounts of space. This does not matter. The important thing is to look for some recognizable difference between a "yes"—strong "O" ring fingers—and a "no"—weakened "O" ring fingers.

~~~

For the purpose of emotional clearing, you will be testing stimuli (beliefs) that are put forth as statements. One such statement might be "I need other people's help to succeed" or, more succinctly, "I am helpless." You might get even more specific than this, such as with "I am helpless when it comes to making money" or "I am helpless when it comes to men (or women)."

In muscle testing, you will want to make as simple a statement as you can, one that can be answered accurately by a "yes" or a "no." You will not, therefore, want to say, "I am angry at myself for not listening to my intuition." This statement is actually in *three* parts. One, that you are angry; two, that you are angry with yourself; and three, that you know why you are angry (for not listening to your intuition). If you test such a multi-level statement, you will not know which part is getting answered. Therefore, you will want to test "I am angry," then "I am angry at myself," then "I am angry at myself for not listening to my intuition."

Should you choose to incorporate The Emotional Detoxx into your personal growth work, you will want to learn to be very specific with your testing statements, choosing each one deliberately and incrementally. If you are methodical and employ a step by step "whittling down" process toward your body's "truth," you will get remarkably accurate results very quickly.

*Remember that it is not **the truth** that you are after in your testing, but rather an exploration and release of any hidden beliefs **you hold as true** that are not serving you.*

Once a limiting belief is brought to your conscious attention, you will need to do a few things with it. First, you will want to recognize it. Many of our "forgotten" beliefs were buried because they were too painful to accept. Instead of challenging them, we tend to hide from them, and we can timidly remain in hiding for a long time. You need to know that it is now safe to come out and play. This is what The Emotional Detoxx will help you to understand.

~~~

Learning how to address the body so that it reveals its hidden secrets is not as difficult as you might imagine. Once you have mastered the basics of self-testing, it is only a matter of knowing what statements to "put to the body" so that a binary system, a "yes" or a "no" answer, can be used to its maximum advantage. The concept here is simple: In muscle testing, we have a free, reliable, perennially available lie-detector test, which helps us uncover all sorts of subconscious sabotaging energy.

The Emotional Detoxx is so-named because it hurries you through the process of nonessential, nonbeneficial (toxic) belief discovery and release (*á la* Michelangelo's stone) and back to your natural (healthy), *essential* self—your "elephant." Throughout the process, you will simultaneously be enhancing and integrating the functions of mind, body, and spirit. I'm continually amazed at the power of this work.

~~~

There is something else you will want to remember regarding "yes" and "no" answers. When you test for nonsupportive beliefs, you are not always looking for a weak response. For example, if you were to test "I believe the world is a dangerous place," you would actually get a "yes"—a *strong* response—and be unable to separate your "O" ring fingers if that happened to be one of your body-conscious beliefs. Your fingers will only weaken when the statement that you have just made is untrue *for you* at your deepest levels. In other words, if you were to test the statement, "I love myself" and got a weakening of the "O" ring fingers, you would know that you had a subconscious self-sabotaging tiger by the tail and some important, liberating work ahead of you. At long last, you are actually able to discover and understand what makes you "tick," what makes you stubbornly and perpetually do the things you do.

Additionally, keep in mind that you are never testing your conscious beliefs, but those that are in your subconscious—your "body beliefs." These may match your conscious beliefs or they may not. Because of this, you may be surprised or even shocked by the responses your body gives you. Trust in the process, and give yourself time to get accustomed to it. The Emotional Detoxx will lead you through the deepest, darkest wilds of your subconscious—through the jungle of your lost, forgotten feelings—till you are face to face with some amazing emotional hidden treasure.

-20- | The Thing Itself

One of the more fascinating aspects of this work is that you can start virtually anywhere with it and still uncover the causal subconscious beliefs that are running you. Let's begin with something fairly simple, shall we? How about a stomachache? You could, however, once you have mastered this marvelously simple technique, proceed from almost any feeling, condition, or belief.

Follow each statement below with an "O" ring muscle test:

Look for the cause:

—My stomach hurts *because* of something I ate. Test: "yes" or "no." (It is "yes" if the "O" ring fingers stay strong, maintaining integrity, "no" if they weaken, due to a momentary interruption of the normal functioning of the nervous system.) If "no," test another idea. If "yes," find out what it was. Let's say it is "no."

—O.K., my stomach hurts because of a resisted emotion. Test: "yes" or "no." If "yes," proceed with the following statements to help you narrow the field of emotional possibilities. If it is "no," test another idea (i.e., because of a belief that I have). Let's say it is "yes." Interestingly, I think you will find that resisted emotion and subconscious belief cause almost all of your "imbalances."

Look for the resisted emotion:

—The *emotion that I'm resisting* is anger. Test: "yes" or "no." Again, let's say it tests "yes." But, if "no," test another idea. (Resentment, hopelessness, guilt, vulnerability, confusion, low self-esteem, disgust, grief, sorrow, being "stuck," irritation, and fear are some other possible choices. You could also say, "Related to my stomachache, I'm stuck" or "Related to my stomachache, I'm confused," etc.)

Look for the family tie:

—The pain in my stomach is *related to* my family. Test: "yes" or "no." If "yes," continue. If "no," test another idea. You could try: mother, father, brother, sister, aunt, uncle, grandmother, etc., even a teacher or boss—anyone within emotional earshot of you. Let's say mother tests "yes."

Look for the life area:

—This anger is related to "fun." Test: "yes" or "no." If "yes," continue. If "no," test another idea. The resisted emotion could also be related to: my job (career, money), love, God, spirituality, religion, my purpose, health, relaxation, feelings of self-worth, self-empowerment, self-expression, sex, or a variation on any of the above themes. Let's say "fun" tests "yes."

Look for the origin:

—The start of this "anger related to fun" was (begin with "pre-conception," then "conception to birth," then "birth to five," "five to ten," "ten to fifteen," "fifteen to twenty," and so on). Narrow this down as much as you can. Let's say this tests "seven years old."

Start putting the pieces together:

If it helps to think of yourself at the age you discover, do so. If not, just keep it in the back of your mind as you test.

—When Mom asked me to visit her this weekend, I wish I had said that I had things I wanted to do for myself (fun). Test: "yes" or "no." If "yes," continue. If "no," test another idea. Say it is "yes."

—I am *angry*. It tests "yes." I am angry with myself. "Yes." I am angry with myself for not standing up to my mother. "Yes" again.

Start testing your beliefs that might underlie this anger:

—I can't say "no" to my mother. Test: "yes" or "no." If "yes," continue. If "no," test another idea. Say it is "yes."

—I believe that if I say "no" to my mother she will stop loving me. Test: "yes" or "no." If "yes," continue. If "no," test another idea. Again, it tests "yes."

—I am only loved if I am "good." Test: "yes" or "no." If "yes," continue. If "no," test another idea. It tests "yes," again.

—I am "bad." Test: "yes" or "no." If "yes," continue. If "no," test another idea. "Yes," again.

—I pretend in order to get my mother's affection. Test: "yes" or "no." If "yes," continue. If "no," test another idea. Another "yes."

—I don't deserve the things I want. I have to bargain for them. "Yes" and "yes" again.

What type of person would think these things?

—I'm: an unimportant person/someone who doesn't count/a person who is not good enough/an unlovable person/a bad person/a phony, etc. Test: "yes" or "no." If "yes," continue. If "no," test another idea. Once more, you get some "yeses" . . . maybe on all counts.

~~~

At this point, make the statement, "I need to know more before I can let my anger and these beliefs go." Test: "yes" or "no." Having done this much belief work, you might have gotten to a "root" issue and, regarding *this* emotional weed at least, may not have to dig any deeper. If you get a "yes," however, keep going by coming up with even more "labels" to describe the kind of person who would feel and think these things (i.e., weak, insecure, etc.).

Assuming that you get a "no," all you need do now is go back over everything that you just uncovered. Give yourself the "gift" of accepting the statements that tested "Yes", not as "true," but as having been true for *you*. This will entail your *feeling* what they have meant to you over the years, not simply giving these discoveries lip service. You may do some crying or ranting or "guilting" for awhile. But that is exactly what you will need to do if you are to release yourself from the vise-like grip these resisted emotions and beliefs have had on you.

If you were to do the above work and felt what each discovery meant to you, you would definitely shift out of resistance and into greater flow. After you have done your feeling work, you would want to go back and retest the emotions and beliefs that you found. If you had faithfully followed each step, these feelings and beliefs should now test negative. Having been discovered, expressed, and released, they should no longer be held, resistant, in your body.

In much this way, once you have learned that you can trust your body's information, you will be able to get to the root of your deepest fears, anxieties, limiting beliefs, and self-sabotaging behaviors. Muscle testing can reveal everything from the cause of a stomachache to the origin of, and remedy for, all types of relationship problems, financial conditions, feelings of anxiety, chronic depression, disease, or a host of other emotional concerns. In other words, all sorts of self-sabotaging energy.

Although much of the evidence testifying to the efficacy of The Emotional Detoxx is still anecdotal, the preponderance of early and continued success clearly confirms its validity. Scientific double-blind studies, though helpful, cannot be undertaken in an area where causation and cure are so unquestionably personal. But there really is no pressing need for such study, not in light of the fact that I have never seen a single negative side effect to the technique. My own story of recovery from chronic asthma, depression, and obsessive/compulsive behavior is as remarkable as it is true.

This work is effective because it allows you to explore the contents of your body-conscious belief systems and to feel and to heal your subconscious pain. The reason this is so important is that these "hidden" energies would otherwise remain undiscovered, but would forever rule you in their omnipotent fashion. They would, if left unchallenged, continue to dictate what you feel, what you choose, and, therefore, nearly everything that you experience—all according to their grossly limited perspective.

-21-   From Oy to Joy

As good as some motivational and personal growth systems first appear, all too often they prove about as effective as a Band-Aid on a gaping wound. At best, many create only a would-be giant, destined to endlessly and precariously roam the earth through an emotional mine field.

Why will The Emotional Detoxx work when other methods disappoint? *Because your trapped feelings are matched up with their original **causal** energetic circumstances.* To get off the therapy/self-help book/personal growth seminar treadmill— to get, as I like to say, from oy to joy—you have got to "come clean." You must emotionally clean house—on a body-conscious level. That is exactly what this work helps you do.

To better understand this, think about a person who seems angry all the time. They appear to be a bottomless pit of anger, disappointment, frustration, and bitterness. With all the venom that they spew, you'd think that they would run out. But they do not. It just keeps on coming. There is a source anger that is perpetually regenerating itself which must be discovered, tapped, and expressed before that "angry" person can finally be free of what seems their intrinsic, perennial fuming. Until the *source* anger is identified and expressed, all the angry tirades in the world will not wrestle the "ick" away.

People who can express their feelings *when they first feel them* do not suppress or harbor them. If you missed your chance the first time around, your only option now is to energetically return to "the scene of the crime" and give yourself consent to feel what you, for one reason or another, originally resisted feeling.

Below is a list for you to reference as you test for feelings and emotions that you may have suppressed. It's safe to say that I could have overlooked some feelings of yours, so please add to this list if you wish. Additionally, it will save you time if you test the emotions in bold type first. These are primary and are more apt to be involved. If no primary emotion or feeling tests "yes," test the secondary emotions, those in regular typeface.

Angry, Irrational, Frustrated, Put-upon, Enraged, Envious.

Resentful, "Poor me" attitude, Stubborn, Bitter.

Vulnerable, Too sensitive, Abandoned, Lost, "Canary in a coal mine" feeling.

Confused, Paranoid.

Indifferent, Numb, Apathetic, Exhausted, Unresponsive.

Shocked, Guilty, Overwhelmed.

Inadequate, Impotent, Helpless, Not enough, Rejected, Powerless, Needy.

Disgusted, Out of control, Fed-up, Feeling "unclean."

Grief stricken, Hopeless, Sad, Silently suffering, Gloomy.

Stuck, Defensive, Stoic, Unmovable, "Righteous."

Irritated, Timid, Uncertain, Doubtful, Shy, Indecisive, Ambivalent.

Afraid, Anxious, Apprehensive, Panicked, Terrified.

To self-test, review the information from the previous two chapters and follow the outline on the next few pages. And, by all means, have fun with this. Setting yourself free ought not be drudgework.

Self-Testing Outline

1. **Create a relaxed, neutral state within you:** Focus on your breath for a few minutes or use any meditation or relaxation technique you like. This is an important step. Accuracy in your testing will be directly proportionate to your ability to relinquish attachment to its outcome. You will color your answers if you care too much what they are. The trick here, as it is in so many areas of life, is to not take things personally. Then your testing (and you) will be just fine.

2. **Put all of your attention on a feeling, doubt, or life condition.** How does it *feel?* Amplify it and experience it fully. Keep your attention here.

3. **Find the resisted emotion:** Say, "I have an emotion in resistance related to this." If "yes," test emotions below. Say, "I'm (i.e., angry) related to this." If no emotion tests "yes," say, "I have a nonbeneficial belief related to this." If this tests "yes," skip the emotions for now and ask yourself, "What would I have to believe to feel this way?" Then proceed from Step 4 on, substituting "belief" for "feeling." If no emotion tests "yes," it could mean that you are not yet ready to go that deep. In this case, work with your beliefs first—your resisted emotions will soon reveal themselves to you.

Emotions and feelings for which you can test:

Angry, Irrational, Frustrated, Put-upon, Enraged, Envious.
Resentful, "Poor me" attitude, Stubborn, Bitter.
Vulnerable, Too sensitive, Abandoned, Lost, "Canary in a coal mine" feeling.
Confused, Paranoid.
Indifferent, Numb, Apathetic, Exhausted, Unresponsive.

Shocked, Guilty, Overwhelmed.
Inadequate, Impotent, Helpless, Not enough, Rejected,
    Powerless, Needy.
Disgusted, Out of control, Fed-up, Feeling "unclean."
Grief stricken, Hopeless, Sad, Silently suffering, Gloomy.
Stuck, Defensive, Stoic, Unmovable, "Righteous."
Irritated, Timid, Uncertain, Doubtful, Shy, Indecisive,
    Ambivalent.
Afraid, Anxious, Apprehensive, Panicked, Terrified.

4. **Test a Life Area:** "This **emotion (X)/feeling** is related to":

My Job/Career/Money	My mission/Purpose
Love	Health
Spirituality/Religion/God	Personal Power/Authority
Fun/Joy	Sex/Creativity
Family	Women/Men/Friends (Other?)

5. **Test the Origin:** "The start of this (i.e., anger related to sex) was": Prior to conception, conception to birth, under age 5, under age 10, under age 15, (etc.). When you find the age range, see if you can narrow it down to the exact age.

6. **Test the Relationship:** "This (feeling) connected to (life area) beginning age "X" is related to my": Mother, Father, Sibling, Friend, Son, Daughter, Teacher, Relative, Boss, (Someone?).

7. **"What would I have to believe to feel (X) related to (person Y)?" It may help to depersonalize this by asking, "What would someone need to believe for them to feel this way?"** Soul-search. List and test as many beliefs as you can that would "support" this feeling. Note the ones that test "yes."

8. **"What type of person would think these things?"** Say, "I am, i.e., a child, a weak person, a bad person, a selfish person, frightened, unlovable, pathetic, naive, etc." Test each one. Several may test "yes." Keep track of those that do.

9. **Say, "I need to know more before I can let this go." Or you could test, "There are more beliefs that I need to uncover before I can let this go" or "There is another emotion related to this."** Test. If "yes," either stay with Step 8 or (if another emotion tests "yes") proceed from Step 3 once again until Step 9 finally tests "no."

   Put your attention on *everything* you have just discovered—all the beliefs, the feelings, the origin, and the relationships. Though on some level you may have always been aware of these things *individually*—in a disjointed way—the power of this work is in the putting of all the pieces together, finally finishing the puzzle, so to speak, so you can put it away.

   Feel everything as completely as you can. Spend several minutes in the realm of this heretofore-banished experience. What does it feel like to be a (fill in the blank) person who believes X, Y, and Z. Really get into it, head to toe. Let every cell of your body feel what this feels like. Surrender to it. If you sense resistance, let that be a part of the feeling as well. Invite all of your feelings to the party, especially those that you have feared the most or are the least proud of. *The more emotion you allow yourself to experience now, the more you will let go.*

10. **When the feelings begin to subside despite your desire to summon them**—Retest everything that tested "yes" to make sure that it was fully *expressed* and is no longer being *suppressed* within you.

Practice is key when it comes to The Emotional Detoxx. If you don't let frustration with your early attempts stop you, you will eventually find that you are a master of this life-changing tool.

-22- | It's Elementary
            My Dear Reader

Another key to letting go of your emotionally charged self-sabotaging behavior lies within the mysterious realm of the ancient *Chinese Five-Element Theory.* According to this remarkable philosophy, you store resisted emotion inside your body, organ specifically.

This means that if you resist feelings of anger, that energy does not simply evaporate, but buries itself deep within you, specifically, in your liver. The same goes for fear (kidney); grief (lungs); guilt (heart); feelings of inadequacy (spleen/pancreas); confusion (thyroid); disgust (stomach); irritation (bladder), resentment (gallbladder); feelings of vulnerability (small intestine); and defensiveness (large intestine). Whenever an emotion is unexpressed, some part of you takes the hit. When an organ or gland is compromised as a result of this repressed energy, its corresponding meridian line will show signs of this compromise as an energetic imbalance. It is this body-knowledge that something is "off," that you give voice and meaning to in your testing.

~~~

According to Eastern wisdom, your body and it's energetic systems break down into five basic categories. The ancient Chinese named these the **Wood Element, Fire Element, Earth Element, Metal Element,** and **Water Element.** There has been much written on **The Five Element Theory,** and you are invited to investigate further. But you will not need to know much more than what follows to have use of this remarkable system for your emotional release work.

Let's say that I make the statement "Wood is out of balance (related to men; or not getting that job; or this anxious feeling that I have; etc.)" and I muscle test it—and it tests "yes." In doing so I have narrowed the number of emotions and corresponding beliefs that I would need to examine. This is because only certain emotions lie within the energetic domain of each element. This fact will save you a great deal of time in your Emotional Detoxx work.

To use The Five-Element Theory in your testing, follow the Self-Testing Outline on page 95 through Steps 1 and 2. Then, before you proceed to Step 3, state and test "Wood is out of balance related to this." If this tests "no," you would test each remaining element (Fire, Earth, Metal, and Water) until you get a "yes."

Once an element is found to be out of balance, go to Step 3 and test the emotions listed under that element. If no element tests out of balance, it could mean that no element truly *is* out of balance, or it could mean that you are not yet ready for that level of work. In either case, continue with Step 3, looking for a nonbeneficial belief that you might be ready to examine.

If you do indeed rebalance an element which was out of balance, you would want to see if there were any other elements out of balance related to what you were testing. It is probably best, however, not to do too much work in any one sitting. I have found that our bodies only want to process so much information at a time. Muscle testing a statement such as "It is for my highest good to do more release work right now" would let you know if it would be advantageous to continue.

On the following page, with the primary emotions in bold type (those most often involved) and the secondary emotions in plain type, are the elements and their attendant emotions and feelings.

~~~

Wood Element

Angry, Depressed, Irrational, Frustrated, Put upon, Enraged, **Resentful,** Envious, Galled, "Poor me" Attitude, Bitter.

Fire Element

Vulnerable, Too sensitive, Abandoned, Lost, "Canary in a coal mine" feeling, **Confused,** Paranoid, Insecure, **Indifferent,** Numb, Apathetic, Depleted, Exhausted, Emotionless, Shocked, Guilty, Overwhelmed, Heart-broken.

Earth Element

Inadequate, Egotistic, (Big Headed), Entitled, Low Self Esteem, Rejected, Powerless, Hopeless, Needy, Lack of control, Worried, **Disgusted,** Distrustful, Fed-up, "Unclean."

Metal Element

Grief Stricken, Hopeless, Sad, Silently Suffering, Gloomy, **Stuck, Defensive,** Compulsively Neat, Stoic, Unmovable, "Righteous."

Water Element

Irritated, Timid, Uncertain, Doubtful, Shy, Indecisive, Ambivalent, **Afraid, Anxious,** Panicked, Terrified, Feeling of Imminent Doom.

If you first test whether an element is out of balance related to a doubt, feeling or condition you are examining, you are in essence streamlining your evolutionary process—quite literally taking a short-cut to the secret hiding places of your greatest resistance.

~~~

Having said that, here is another approach you could take. Instead of starting with an element and its corresponding emotions, you could begin your Emotional Detoxx by examining a specific life aspect. Most personal issues fall within one of seven basic life categories. These are Relationships, Money, Self-Esteem, Health, Grief/Loss, Spirituality/Faith, and Personal Power. Below is a list of "loaded" belief statements that are purposefully designed to reveal where your emotional work might lie. Don't be upset if none of the following statements test true for you. Believe it or not, most people need major work in every category. Begin your testing by selecting an area of life you wish to examine, make and test the corresponding statements, then begin your Emotional Detoxx from any statement that tests "no."

For instance, if you were to test "I am a good person" from the Self-Esteem category, and it tested "no," you would go to the top of the Self-Testing Outline, and for Step 2, you would use the fact that you didn't believe yourself to be a good person as the doubt/feeling that you would put your attention on.

The following are the seven basic life categories and their corresponding belief statements. If you have trouble getting good results with these, try putting them in the "negative" —i.e., "I am *not* capable of intimacy." However, realize that if you work in the negative form of these statements, a strong muscle response would still indicate a "yes"—yes, I am *not* capable of intimacy.

And please remember, too, that these are just beliefs. Only if they remain unexamined and unchallenged would they necessarily have any bearing on what might actually be "true" or possible.

Relationships

1. I am capable of intimacy.
2. I am ready for intimacy.
3. It's easy for me to love.
4. It's easy for me to be loved.
5. It's easy to be myself in relationships.
6. I accept growth and change in my relationships.
7. I am safe in my relationships with other people.

Money

1. Money is good.
2. I like money.
3. It's easy for me to make money.
4. It's easy for me to spend money.
5. I can make money doing what I love.
6. It's safe for me to have a lot of money.

Self-Esteem

1. I am a good person.
2. I accept myself.
3. I love myself.
4. I am confident.
5. I am comfortable with myself.
6. My best is good enough.
7. I create my own safety.

Health

1. I enjoy having a body.
2. I love my body.
3. I accept health as my natural state.
4. My body has an intelligence of its own.
5. My body heals itself naturally and quickly.
6. I am safe in physical form.

Grief/Loss

1. I give myself consent to feel all my feelings.
2. I accept my grief.
3. I accept life's ups and downs and do not take them personally.
4. I know that no energy is ever created or destroyed—it is only transformed.
5. It's easy for me to Let Go.
6. I know that which is essential to me cannot be taken away.
7. I am safe because there is nothing that is essential *to* me that can be taken *from* me.

Spirituality/Faith

1. I belong here.
2. The power that created everything created me.
3. That which created me sustains me.
4. That which created me is within me.
5. All is God.
6. I am an essential part of All-That-Is.
7. I am safe/loved/enough/good/worthy, etc., because I am God as (your name here).

Personal Power

1. I am able.
2. I trust myself.
3. I honor my ideas.
4. I am divinely inspired.
5. I enjoy personal growth and change.
6. The best "me" I can be is the most "me" I can be.
7. I am safe because I am Me.

A "no" to any of the above statements (or "yes" to its negation) is a portal to a personal growth adventure. If you embrace this work and do not take any of it too personally, you will be well on the way to Let Go.

-23- To Self-Test Or Not To Self-Test?

The purpose of *When You Reach the End of Your Rope, Let Go!* is to give you as much autonomy in the area of self-help as possible. After all, self-help really could mean *self*-help. However, it has been suggested, and I would agree, that not everyone is interested in learning to muscle test him- or herself. With this in mind, I will momentarily step down off my soapbox and suggest a team approach to the Emotional Detoxx.

Admittedly I have a practice wherein I guide clients through the breakdown, breakthrough, and recovery work that is outlined throughout these pages. Sessions typically travel to the very same psycho/emotional/spiritual destinations you will travel as you advance through this book. When it comes to the actual muscle testing, however, I act as a facilitator for my client. In other words, I muscle test them as they do their discovery work. Then, when they have gathered all the information necessary from the ground of their body-consciousness and have done their feeling work, I retest them to make sure that they have expressed (Let Go) what had previously been suppressed.

By the same token, you could do your Emotional Detoxx work with a partner. Instead of muscle testing yourself, someone else could test you. There are some differences which must be understood before you proceed. As opposed to self-testing, where a weakening of the "O" Ring fingers indicates a "no," when working with a partner we have a weakening of the testee's arm. And instead of being unable to separate the "O" Ring fingers, indicating a "yes" when self-testing, when working with a partner the testee's arm will remain strong.

Here are some ground rules to follow to help ensure accurate testing:

—Both the tester and testee should stand facing each another.

—Neither should be smoking, eating, drinking anything but water, or chewing gum. Neither should be preoccupied or distracted in any way. Both should completely be committed to the process.

—The testee's outstretched left arm (test arm) should be held parallel to the floor, elbow locked, palm down, and at a 45 degree angle (midway between straight left and straight ahead.)

—There should be no eye contact between you. The testee could look down or slightly off to the right.

—Both the tester and the testee need to clear their minds as much as possible. Exercise no judgements or expectations.

—The tester places his right hand on top of the testee's left wrist.

—When testing the integrity (strength) of the testee's arm, the tester will say, "Hold" prior to each test. In that way, the two of you can get your timing synchronized.

—Prior to doing any actual work, you should practice. After saying, "Hold," the tester will want to press down on the testee's wrist. The testee should resist the tester with equal force, meaning he will not want to fight him, but will simply want to try and remain unmovable.

—As with the self-testing procedure, begin by practicing on something simple and knowable. The testee should state his first name: "My name is ____." The tester should say, "Hold" and apply just enough pressure downward so as to try and move the testee's arm downward. If the testee uses his real name and he is aligned with his name, the tester, using moderate force, should not be able to push the testee's arm down. Next, the testee should deliberately choose a name which is not his own: "My name is ____." This time when the tester says, "Hold" and pressure is applied to the wrist of the testee's outstretched arm, the testee's arm should weaken and the tester should be able to discern the difference between what is "yes" for the testee (strong response) and what is "no" (weak response). Keep practicing until the right pressure and timing is achieved, and a "yes" and a "no" are discernable by the tester.

—Before beginning The Emotional Detoxx, have the testee state, "I give my consent to do this work and recognize that it is for my highest good." The tester will want to say, "Hold" immediately following this statement (as with all statements the testee makes) and apply the amount of pressure downward he has learned works from his previous practicing. If the testee's arm stays strong, you may begin. If not, you would want to consider testing at another time.

~ ~ ~

At this point in your reading you might want to practice doing some Emotional Detoxx work. Then again, you might prefer to read on before diving in. Don't be upset if you are still unconvinced of the merits of this work and want to know more. That is what experimentation is for, and that is why there is a Part Two.

Whether you self-test or work with a partner, remember that personal evolution is a process of incremental gain. Give yourself time to explore and experiment with your new tools, and reread those sections describing the technique several times before you have a go at it.

Part Two:

From Skeptic To Mystic

I have lived on the lip of insanity
Wanting to know reasons
Knocking at the door
It opens.
I've been knocking from the inside.

Rumi

-24- | Me, Again

As a young boy, I would gaze out into the starry nighttime sky through befuddled, fledgling eyes. Instead of allowing myself wonder, exhilaration, and awe, I would torture myself and rack my bewildered brain, attempting to comprehend the impossible. Contemplating infinity was always good for a total mind-warp. As I stared out at the heavens from that grassy hilltop in the far northern reaches of Westchester County, New York, I would wrestle with the nature of endlessness . . . .

My young mind struggled as it attempted to wrap itself around that unwieldy notion. Dizzy, desperate, yet defiant, I would go at it from another angle. I would ask myself, "O.K., suppose there is an end to that sky out there, then what? What would the border be made of, and what, pray tell, would be on the other side of that 'end'?" I was getting nowhere, fast. But I wasn't finished yet.

I began to ponder the pieces of my puzzlement. With my trusty telescope that I had feverishly unwrapped one Hanukkah/Christmas morning, I reached into our solar system and beyond, into worlds millions of years old. The light from these distant galaxies had literally taken aeons to arrive at my wide-eyed fascination. I saw moons circling planets, and planets circling suns. Standing in the icy dark of a late December snow, my adolescent brain reeled in wonder.

For my next birthday, I asked for a microscope . . . .

Hours upon hours would pass as I then peered down into worlds so tiny, that to the naked eye they didn't seem to exist at all. But these were worlds nonetheless, teeming with color and motion. I was awed by the power of the electron microscope, capable of penetrating even tinier regions. I searched for some clue, some hint of meaning, some answer that could calm my growing inner chaos.

Traces in a cloud chamber spoke of subatomic levels, "implying" protons, electrons, neutrons, and quarks. I say "implying," because, to my knowledge, these particles are so minute that no one has ever actually seen them. Yet there they were just the same, sub-miniature worlds microcosmically mirroring the moons, planets, and suns; and these, their gigantic cosmic counterparts, macrocosmically mirroring them back.

Not only did it seem as though some fantastic intelligence was at work, but stylistically, from a design perspective, there was definitely a continuation of "motif." The Oneness of everything was startling to me. "As above, so below." "As within, so without." *Incredible.* Even the great space between celestial bodies is known to be proportionately similar amid electrons, protons, and neutrons of atoms within what appear "solid" materials.

I felt as though I was hot on the trail of something—but what, I had no idea.

The uniform nature of nature itself, from those things most colossal to those things most minute, fascinated me, yet I could not fathom the significance nor concede the coincidence. The clues were mounting steadily but my state of mind seemed to be getting worse and worse. The more information I gathered, the more confused I became. Mine was a runaway curiosity, frighteningly unstoppable.

~ ~ ~

I now realize that my need to know that which defied understanding was just one more attempt at trying to create a feeling of safety. However, it led me headlong into a frantic, futile search. I would go to bed at night mulling over thoughts like: "When I think to myself, '*I'm* going to school tomorrow,' and mother thinks to *her*self, '*I'm* going to the grocery store in the morning,' her 'I,' to her, and my 'I,' to me, 'feel' the same to us, respectively." We are, my thinking went, made essentially of the same original "stuff," or as I would later describe it, individualized points of a mutual, perpetual, intelligent Energy Source.

This "I-ness," this sense of "I," I understood to be different than my sense of "me." This becomes an important distinction, so allow me to explain. "I" I defined as my primary, authentic, active sensation of my essential "Self." "Me" I characterized as something more conditional: the reflected and, therefore, secondary "self-concept." It was frightening for me to consider what was beginning to appear undeniable . . . What seemed to differentiate me from everyone else was my limited self-concept. By removing the layers of conditioning supplying that concept, I would, in essence, be stepping into a universal sense of myself in which "I," as I knew "me," could simply vanish!

The choice was terrifying: Either stay with the familiar, finite, *known*, small sense of myself (where I was truly unhappy), or abandon "me," my conditioned self, in hopes of experiencing my "I," my essential Self. I was much too young and far too inexperienced to consider such a choice even for a minute, and so my search for identity and "wholeness" would, by necessity, remain outwardly directed, and therefore quite futile, for some time to come.

~~~

My grip on reality, whatever *that* was, was beginning to get far too loose for comfort. I'm sure that having been born and raised an identical twin intensified my need and early search for personal identity. However I witness this "thirst" in others in my practice regularly, and it appears to be a universal phenomenon. I merely had a head start in dealing with it, due to the acute nature of my pressing identity issues.

Unbeknownst to me at the time, I was knee-deep in the early stages of becoming a modern-day Parsifal. This mythological medieval Knight of the Round Table, who went on a Grail quest, represents our frustrating search for inner peace and purpose. The trumpets of the elusive Grail castle called to my frightened young spirit. To own this mythical sense of well-being, I was sure that I needed to be privy to some great universal secret, to answer some Sphinx's riddle, or something. I just *knew* that the answer had to be "out there" somewhere.

In his provocative and illuminating work *He*, Robert A. Johnson clarifies the nature of the glorious Grail castle experience: "It doesn't exist in physical reality. It is an inner reality, a vision, poetry, a mystical experience, and it cannot be found in any outer place. To search for it outwardly is to exhaust one's self and to court discouragement."[6]

Precisely. But I did not know this. And the truth of it would continue to elude me for years to come.

In the meantime, I was in the midst of a furious outward search—turning to friends, books, and gurus of all kinds—not yet able to recognize that the treasure, the magic, and that diabolically elusive "place" for which I searched, was inside me—that it *was* me. I still felt a long, long way from "home."

~~~

My teens were proving to be excruciatingly difficult. I was, to put it mildly, in way over my head. I thought constantly, learning daily and first-hand-the-hard-way, the limitations inherent in skeptically analyzing everything. I was always an idea away from the "thing" itself, forever in an intellectually filtered, itemized, calculated, symbolic representation of whatever original event was actually going on around me. The Grail castle was always just over the next hill. I felt this distance. My sense of "I," my primary, authentic, active sensation of my essential "Self," was painfully unreconciled and unrealized. Though it ultimately proved to be only a matter of perspective, the gap between "me," my conditional self, and "I," my essential Self, felt immense, and it seemed to be getting wider by the day.

I was drowning in emotional turmoil. I loathed my lack of spontaneity, my sense of separateness. Soon a terrible feeling of "aloneness" began to close in on me. I became deeply, deeply troubled—so much so, that by my twenty-first birthday, I had buried myself under the avalanche of a painful nervous breakdown. Panic attacks were now not only a daily affair, they were continuous. Not only was I unable to work, I couldn't even leave the house. Sleep and television were my only escape from incessant, acute anxiety.

I remember conducting an experiment with the television set. I would be watching a show, experiencing some relief, when I would deliberately turn my gaze from the set for a moment. Almost instantly, a flood of intense fear would overwhelm me. When I would return my attention to the set, I would feel almost instant relief. This was some of the first hard evidence I had uncovered that my thinking was directly linked to my pain— magically, though temporarily, calmed by the diversion the television provided.

Despite this discovery, I could no longer cope. My questioning, "in my head" approach to living was finally giving out; life was caving in on me. I became a terrified, depressed, lonely, anxiety-ridden mass of confusion.

Oh boy, recounting all of this makes me really glad to be where I am today. It also reminds me of a rather relevant personal story that I began writing, a long, long time ago . . . .

| "The Boy and the Hill"

What follows is a short story that I started to write when I was fourteen years old. Over the course of the next three decades, I would pick it up and "tweak it" every now and then. Though I played with syntax and word substitution, the "plot" has remained faithful to the original draft.

The story of "The Boy and the Hill" traveled with me from New York, to college in Indiana, then to Chicago, then to Los Angeles, mysteriously remaining one of my most precious possessions. As a high school freshman, I had no idea why these particular words came through. In retrospect, it is clear that here were the stirrings of my Grail search.

One of the more fascinating and rewarding aspects of developing an awareness of mythology is to then have the ability to watch as the myth unfolds within us; even if, as in this case, it spans over a quarter of a century and travels an entire continent.

On a cold afternoon, late in a winter day, a small boy trudged up Overlook Mountain Road; his sleigh, fastened to a rope clenched tightly in his hand, trailed behind him. He was alone.

As was often the case on those chilly, dreary afternoons, he would hike up to the very top of the hill, as much for the beautiful view that awaited him there, as for the sensational ride back down. But today, somehow, felt different. Today, as he climbed and looked around him, nothing seemed to move; not a man, nor a car—not even the snow usually swept by the unending wind. "How strange," he thought, nearing the top of the hill. "It's like a perfect picture, and I'm *in* the picture and somehow watching it, too."

As he continued to climb, the boy counted the number of houses he passed. Just beyond the twelfth home, he reached the summit and fixed his sleigh sideways, so he could sit and face the rooftops, the woods, and the church steeple that glimmered in the distance.

There were no birds singing, no men out shoveling their driveways, and no children building snowmen in their yards. There was only he, the boy, woolen capped and gloved—alone—perched atop his sleigh, overlooking it all. There he rested, elbow to knee, cheek to fist, and let out a deep sigh. The crisp winter air filled his lungs, and the icy wind whispered in his ears.

The hill, the wind, and the cold began to hypnotize him, and as the boy stared out across the vast white valley, he began fantasizing that what he saw before him was all that comprised the universe, and he, its sole guardian.

~~~

After a time, the boy could not feel the cold at his face, nor could he hear the wind as it howled through his woolen cap. His eyes, which had now tightened to an icy stare, slowly scanned about their frozen domain in searchlight fashion.

For what seemed an eternity, he watched over his land, now gone white to gray—appearing eerie, cold, and hostile—even to its sole sentinel.

Then something strange began to happen. Questions of meaning and purpose began to rattle in the boy's head. Hundreds of questions, thousands of questions; questions screaming by so fast that they began to blur into one gigantic "WHY?" Then, slowly, from parts he didn't even know that he had, feelings of power and uniqueness began to well up from deep within him. These were no ordinary, everyday feelings. So intense were they, that the feelings electrified him, frightening the boy to his core.

Then suddenly, and as inexplicably as they had arrived, the questions and the feelings were gone. As surely as these had taken control of him, they had vanished, leaving nothing but teary eyes and a pounding heart.

~~~

Against the darkening sky, smoke from a nearby chimney caught the boy's attention. The air had grown exceptionally cold, and porch light from each of the twelve homes began its slow fade onto the slope. He rose and turned his sleigh toward the bottom of the hill. His body ached, and his hands were cold and stiff.

Looking out across the treetops, he no longer felt alone. It was strange, too, because there were still no birds singing, no men shoveling driveways, and no children building snowmen in their yards. It was a feeling not easily described—a moment when earth, sky, and self seemed to "harmonize." Within this interlude, the boy became wise and somehow knew that he, too, belonged.

~~~

Letting the sleigh glide a bit, he followed behind, then leaped on belly first. The wind at his cheeks once more felt refreshing, and the crisp winter air again filled his lungs. Hands at either side of the steering bar regained their feeling, and the wood beneath them felt wonderful and somehow very "real," despite his woolen gloves.

Twelve driveways later, the sleigh came to a slow gliding stop alongside a row of mailboxes. The boy dismounted, stood, and quickly unfastened the rope from between the boards at the back of the sleigh. It was now very dark, for there was no moon, yet the snow seemed to reflect a hint of light. He wondered for a moment where the light might be coming from. Then, with a shrug of his little shoulders, the boy simply put it out of his mind, leaving his curiosity in the snow behind him. After all, he was cold, tired, and hungry, and these were far more important matters that now required his attention.

In a few minutes, he was nearly home, sniffing at the dinnertime air, pulling rhythmically at his faithful winter companion. With high, deliberate steps, his boots cut through the icy snow, sending crunching echoes through the surrounding silence.

Behind him, in a cold and silent darkness, broken only by an occasional porch light, stood twelve homes on a hill, where no birds sung, no men shoveled their driveways, and no children built snowmen in their yards.

~~~

It gives me great joy to revisit this story, because I think I finally understand what it was trying to tell me all along. In simple parable, it neatly travels in minutes to a "place" that would ultimately take me over twenty years to find. I now believe that the tale of "The Boy and the Hill" came to me as my Awareness—or what I used to call "my third-person perspective"—attempted to head off the need for a difficult and painful quest for personal identity.

The little boy on the hill (me, if you hadn't guessed it), in viewing that perfect winter wonderland before him, begins to sense that, although he is unique, he, too, is part of something greater. Something, perhaps, in which he could begin to trust. But this is much too large a concept for the boy to grasp. And so he is involuntarily thrown into an experience that he cannot fathom, much as a nonswimmer might be thrown into the ocean and told to sink or swim.

I did eventually swim, but not without a great deal of preliminary flailing about and one near-fatal drowning.

-26- The Boy Gets Buoyant

I didn't realize it at the time, but it was precisely *because* I was forced to relax my perpetual thinking, my need to "know," that I could at long last begin an *experientially* based life. This change was imposed by the brutal isolation and otherwise oppressive nature of my breakdown. No longer would I, nor *could* I, question that which seemed without answer. Finally, out of necessity, I began to trust my personal sense of things on a moment-to-moment basis. It was either trust or bust, and there was still plenty of living I wanted to do—despite the emotional pain and upheaval. From this point forward, I began to develop the muscles and the philosophy of a Thought Farmer and to understand the need for an Emotional Detoxx.

~~~

It is precisely at this juncture, my brave friend, where you may now stand. And just like Parsifal—who finally only needed to ask, "Who does the Grail serve?"—all you need do is ask some well-formulated questions—to wonder, even briefly, "Where is the light coming from?" It seems that neither he nor we were ever expected to have the answers, only the courage to ask, the willingness to accept, and the openness wherein answers might reveal themselves to us, *through* us, as some sort of inner and unique resonance.

We ask, until we learn that our questions are already being answered, but in a language other than the one we were expecting to hear. If we question with our hearts, we must also be willing to listen with them for the answers. We must augment the search that we have begun with our minds and employ the rest of our sensory and extra-sensory equipment. **We've been looking for diamonds with a metal-detector.** If we are ever to recapture experience, we have got to be in an experiential mode, not an analytical one.

~~~

Suppose that you go to the beach in search of a good time—an experience of fresh ocean air and warm sunshine. Knowing the scientific composition of sunlight or the physics behind the tide's response to lunar pull won't improve your mood as you attempt to soak in all that nature. An inherent trust in the "goodness" of the sun and a sense of communion with the water, warm wind, and sky are, however, factors that could raise your sunbathing to the level of "enjoyment." These are attitudinal, inner conditions, and they are essential to the inner process of joy. One analytical "eye" on the possibility of overexposure to the sun would serve, but not throughout, for it would squeeze every drop of pleasure from these otherwise pleasant moments.

A good helping of "letting go" (unanalyzed, nonjudged, unfiltered "beingness"), coupled with an ounce of prevention (a moment of common sense), seems to provide a healthy, workable balance. We do not want to dismiss the mind altogether. We simply want to employ it for what it does best—analyze, calculate, and decision-make. Otherwise, we want it to relax, because beyond this, it simply gets in the way.

~~~

Most of us are longing for a sense of inner-peace. We wish to have our own Grail castle experience. We simply want to feel "good." This is unquestionably doable. To accelerate the attainment of tranquility and joy, you can begin to seek not just an experience of belonging, but a certainty of it. Let your mind, with its incredible powers of perception and analysis, really do a job for you.

When you can end your anxiety, you can begin your living.

Consider the nature of cellular regeneration. If you cut your finger, the wound heals. *Unbelievable.* If this, in and of itself, isn't cause for trust in a union with a greater intelligence, then I don't know what would be. You periodically need to remind yourself how literally fantastic life is, and get out of the habit of taking your "miracles" for granted.

How about the magic you work every minute of every day, as you breathe in life-giving oxygen offered to you by your friends, the trees? Don't look now, but this really is Mr. Rodgers' neighborhood. You have a wondrous symbiotic relationship with the "greens" of the world. They provide oxygen to you by using your carbon dioxide "waste" in their essential process of photosynthesis. You use their "waste" oxygen, essential in your process of respiration, and return the carbon dioxide (and the favor) back to them . . . et cetera, et cetera, et cetera. A perfect system. One man's waste fills another man's need.

Talk about Oneness. Whether it is the biosphere, gravity, sunlight, friendly bacteria, earthworms, the food chain, or any other aspect of our amazing ecosystem, there is balance and belonging. It's time to give yourself the same consideration you do the earthworm, and accept—and never doubt—that there is a place here for you, too.

Spend some time with this fundamental stuff. It can be cause for great peace.

~~~

So what does all this mean? That you shouldn't worry? That you don't need to constantly concern yourself with one thing after another in order to ensure that your life turns out the way you want it to? Correct. **Worry kindles the flames of the very fires you fear most**. Worry sabotages. It is counterproductive energy.

"How can I stop worrying?"—this is a question I would ask myself thousands of times. The universe's very poetic answer to me was this: "As there is wisdom in the rosebud that allows it eventual full bloom; so, too, is there wisdom within you, which, if allowed its graceful, unencumbered sway, delivers you in full bloom as well."

O.K. . . . la la la, sounds very nice. Only one problem—I'm not a flower. I'm a curious, analytical man; capable, among many other things, of feelings of great doubt, isolation, fear, prejudice, worry, skepticism, and numerous other horrors. Interestingly, I begin to see that my "knowledge of good and evil," my judging and comparing lie central to most of these ill feelings. Right/wrong, good/bad; pretty soon I'm not sure whether or not I should bother to get out of bed in the morning (back to that basic problem).

Robert A. Johnson illumines the nature of this threshold:

> "When a man knows that he is alone, unique and on a solitary quest he will be out of that dark time . . . All psychological suffering (or happiness, taken in its usual sense) is a matter of comparison. When one accepts the solitariness of his journey *there is no comparison possible* (my italics), and he is in that existential world where things simply 'are.' In this realm there is no happiness or unhappiness in the usual sense but only that state of being that is correctly called Ecstasy."[7]

Any of the countless comparisons I am apt to make in hope of choosing "correctly" at any decision point in my life require me to make a judgment—one thing _____er than another. These judgments and comparisons (i.e., "I'm bad," or "He's too this," or "She's too that") invariably limit me in a sort of fixated stupor to some arbitrarily imposed external standard, obscuring what might otherwise be true or possible for me, experientially.

For instance, I have a client who had met a man who she said really intrigued her. "Unfortunately," she reported, "he's my height." She was ready to dismiss this fellow altogether, when I suggested that she suspend her prejudice long enough to see what the original intrigue was all about. It took her days of wrestling with herself before she finally acquiesced, deciding at last to accept a date with what turned out to be a lovely, albeit vertically challenged young man. They are now happily married with three children . . . just kidding.

But seriously, this guy *could* turn out to be a great lover, a true friend, or maybe a terrific business connection. Who knows? My client, who by the way, has a physical and spiritual beauty that she is only now beginning to recognize and accept, was merely projecting her own constant self-deprecating, self-prejudicial thinking out into her world, and finding fault *everywhere*.

Prejudice is life-robbing. It's a reaction to our subconscious feelings of fear and self-hate. If left unchallenged, these judgments will remain constant thorns in the side of the stubbornly naive, willfully ignorant, closed-minded Thought Farmer.

~~~

As far as we know, the rose never questions for an instant that it is a rose. White rose, pink rose, red rose—what does it care? It doesn't say, "Gee, I wish I were a yellow rose. *They* have all the fun." Without self-conscious awareness, the rose is free to unabashedly be its most "whatever color" rose-self. People, on the other hand, seem riddled with self-conscious doubt and fear. We feel: short, stupid, fat, greedy, ugly, poor . . . ad nauseam. These judgments are the products of comparison to some outside standard—each one the remnant of our prejudicial thinking.

How can we—who have supposedly been given dominion over the world's "lesser" life forms—hope to fill the painful void and bridge the great chasm created by the nonstop digging of our judgmental minds? How can we get to be less afraid, and do a little "blooming" ourselves?

Mystic Secret 4: *Worry is what we do instead of doing what we can. It is excuse disguised as concern.* What we worry and complain about, we create.

Exercise 4: Start listening to the things you say to yourself and others. Listen to the tone of your voice and to the pessimistic or optimistic value of it. If you find that you give a lot of lip service to negative sorts of energies, see if you can curb this tendency. Once you understand that what you articulate you create, you may be more interested in changing your tune.

Worry is almost always based on a misguided or false belief. For instance, if you are poor, you might have the belief that there's not enough to go around—what's called a poverty consciousness. Check it out. Run that belief through The Emotional Detoxx. Or just take a good look around you; so many other people have so much. Where did they get it? If you are not generating enough for yourself, you are, without a doubt, believing more in scarcity than abundance—more in limitation than possibility.

You cannot count the number of grains of sand on a beach, nor the number of stars in the sky, nor the number of opportunities you have already let pass you by (don't worry, these are limitless as well). Stop using "lack" as an excuse for not trying. If you are scared, then admit it. That's a whole other story. *That* you can deal with. It would be a shame, however, if you don't admit your fears to yourself and ferret out the truth of the matter.

Use The Emotional Detoxx to explore your hidden fears. You'll find that you are more afraid of your fear than of whatever you thought you were afraid of in the first place. Remember, safety is an inner production, requiring an experiential, nonanalytical approach. Be adventurous and have some courage, and watch your fear dissolve before your very eyes.

-27- The Art of Feeling Good

As alone as you may feel at times in your quest for a sense of "Self," of "well-being," or of "wholeness"—loneliness, that feeling of "separateness" you may experience, is actually only an illusion created by your hitherto cursory take on life. As you look more and more deeply within yourself, you begin to discover that you have a universal center—your essence and perhaps the essence of Life itself—connecting you to all things. But, like Narcissus, who gazed into a pool of water only to fall in love with his own image and die of a broken heart, you too will be struck with but a surface appreciation of yourself, and stuck with your own brand of living-death, if you do not look longer and deeper.

By not delving into our complexities, we are forced to manufacture an inflated self-image. This attempts to compensate us for our lack of self-knowledge and ensuing self-distrust. We assert the opposite of what we fear, as in the case of narcissism—self-importance substitutes for the fear of helplessness or powerlessness. By so doing, the world becomes either friend or foe depending on whether or not it backs us up in our assertions. In terms of successfully travelling down the highway of life, narcissism is an accident waiting to happen.

In spite of all this, there is nothing essentially wrong with narcissism, *per se*. It is simply a good idea gone bad. Narcissism is an extremely young, immature form of self-love. Falling short of its mark, it wreaks all sorts of personal havoc. With narcissism comes the illusion of separateness. We feel disconnected because we have not looked closely enough to realize our belonging. This is a painful way to live life. There is typically a sense of "me against you," a feeling of "not enough," and a sort of claustrophobia—where the world, as big as it is, feels "out there" somewhere, and I'm "in here" somewhere—trapped in my limited sense of myself.

"Separateness" is a fable told to the heart by a frightened ego.

~~~

In narcissism, instead of the experience of belonging, there is one of longing. If this is the feeling you have, you will need to put the "be" back. *Be* with yourself, relax into, and get a feel for who and what you are, essentially—on an experiential level, not an analytical one. Meditation can be key to opening yourself up to this experience. By *being* with yourself, you will be able to turn that sense of longing into one of *be-longing*, and your feelings of aloneness into *all-one-ness*. Through this transition, you then *re-member*, you re-join the *uni-verse*—the one song, and at last find "wholeness"—*holiness*. When we dissect our language in this way, we can truly understand its esoteric meaning. All signs, even our very language, point to Oneness and connection.

Both in my practice and in this book, I tend to harp a bit on meditation. I do so, because it has proven, over centuries of practice, to be an effective tool for cultivating this feeling of "connectedness." Meditation helps us detach ourselves from our habitual and oftentimes judgmental thinking, allowing for a less filtered, more intimate experience of life. I suggest that you get yourself a copy of Jon Kabat-Zinn's *Wherever You Go, There You Are*. Whether you are new to meditation or a veteran, you will come away from this work armed (or I should say disarmed) for Here and Nowness—and far more in touch with the truth about yourself.

Feeling good requires a sense of "connectedness," of belonging, both to ourselves and to our world. This demands a deeper appreciation—actually a remembering—of Who and What we *really* are, and the subsequent release of our belief-based fear. So by all means keep up the exercises.

~~~

In order to truly benefit from a state of universal acceptance, to have the experience that you are "cradled" in the arms of a caring collective, you must yield to it by giving yourself permission to experience something *totally* new. This may seem obvious, but consent of this kind often requires a great deal of soul searching and self-talk. It demands the courage and the discipline to challenge many of your oldest beliefs and feelings, both about yourself and your world. Some of these may feel as much a part of you as do your head and heart. Because of this, challenging what have become your "core" beliefs can be frightening—as if you were engaged in a slow, methodical process of self-annihilation. Stick with your Emotional Detoxx work, and these fears will subside.

His crop may distinguish the farmer. He may live or die by it, but he is *not* it. The Thought Farmer may be distinguished by the quality of his thoughts and feelings—he *will* live and die by them—but again, he is not his thought nor his feeling, nor they he.

Mystic Secret 5: *You are not who you think you are.* Therefore, don't get too comfortable with your "labels." They can't begin to define you.

Exercise 5: On a clean piece of paper, make a list of every answer you can think of to the question "Who am I?"

Be creative. "The being living in this skin" is just as good an answer as any other. Give this exercise some time and energy. Exhaust your concept of yourself.

For example: I am . . . .

A man	A lover	A good person	An American
A writer	A brother	Me	A human being
A therapist	An uncle	A son	My genetics
Geoffrey Rose	A musician	A friend	My karma

Keep writing until you run out of things that you think you are. Then make a list answering the question, "What negative judgments do I make about myself?"

For example: I am . . . .

Undisciplined	Weak-willed	Vengeful	Too short
Lazy	Unworthy	Self-conscious	Too fat
Scared	Naive	Unacceptable	Too egocentric
Confused	Untalented	Judgmental	Too vain

Write until you run out of answers to these questions. They will help you to know who you *think* you are. The good news is that what is *possible* for you could be a horse of a very different color.

-28- | # I've Gotta Be Me
(Whoever *That* Is)

Learning to identify the "me" from the "not-me" portions of who you are, as basic and essential a process as it is, proves to require near Herculean effort. Or maybe you don't think so, having just come up with such extensive "I am" lists.

Well, let's assume that the process of knowing yourself may not be quite as straightforward as you may have thought, and move to the shallow end of the pool, shall we? Ask yourself, "If I lost my right arm, would I still be me?" Better yet, clip your fingernails, and see if you feel any diminished sense of yourself. It sounds funny, I know, but honestly can you? Do you see where I am headed with this line of thinking? If you change your mind about something, are you still *you*? I think it is safe to say that you are. Well then, where is the *you* in all these accoutrements? Where do you cross the "you/not-you" line? If you can lose whole body parts, and effectively alter the contents of your mind and still be "you," then who *are* "you"?

Because it appears easier to discern that which you are not, rather than define the "who" or "what" that you are, let's work backward from there. You could eliminate: thoughts, attitudes, moods, feelings, beliefs, opinions, nationality, religion, gender, career, appendages, material possessions, friends, lovers, family, hair color, excess body weight, various internal organs, successes and failures, memories, expectations. . . and still essentially be "you." Who on earth are you, then?

Perhaps, if you are none of these "other" things, it is the individualized point of awareness . . . The vantagepoint that you seem to exclusively occupy . . . The "where" from which you are able to recognize all the "not-you" stuff . . . That "place" most infinitely within, that you can conclusively and unequivocally call "You."

Or . . . Maybe this point of awareness that seems so irremovably "you," because it operates under the pretense that there is such an arrangement as a "you/not you" in the first place, artificially generates "things out there" from the sensory input your brain receives. Perhaps it is not that you are none of these "other" things, but that you *are* these things, undifferentiated—the observed simply an arrangement of impulses within you, the observer. Perhaps there is no "you," and no "not you," but only the unison event "Here and Now."

~~~

Yikes! Luckily, understanding is not a prerequisite for magnificence. The sequoia does not have to know what it is, where it came from, or where it is going in order to live two thousand years and reach hundreds of feet into the air. It achieves through an unbridled *experience* of itself.

I could perhaps, and perhaps, and perhaps till the cows come home. Whatever the truth is, it is apt to make about as much sense to you and to me as do the concepts of "infinity" and "eternity"—namely *none*. Whatever "you" are, the experience of "you" is all that will ever actually matter. And whatever that experience is, it is quite malleable, and definable *by* you.

"You," therefore, are a work in progress—a changeling— totally featureless without your sensory equipment, beliefs, feelings, and attitudes to offer you quality. "You" are a pure, undefinable, history-less "zone" that, for all intents and purposes, is waiting for interpretation, waiting for you to breathe your brand of life into it. You are the essence of creation itself and the creation that ensues.

You and I can be the sequoia or we can be the moss growing at its feet. That is what is meant to have free-will. Neither is better. All is life. What type of life we choose is up to us. This sets mankind apart from every other known life form.

~~~

These, my friend, are the foothills of the Land of Enlightenment. To have choice is to be able to decide where you shall intersect the rolling contour of the infinite. As *Anatomy of the Spirit* author Caroline Myss, Ph.D., writes, "Choice is the process of creation itself."[8] How do you navigate, how do you develop your awareness of, this magical, elusive place called Creation? And how do you-as-Thought Farming-alchemist turn life's lead into gold?

One thing you can *easily* do, and that you owe yourself if you are sincere, is to have a regular meditative practice. This is a big part of the "remembering to remember the present" that I mentioned earlier, and it is absolutely foundational for healthy, natural, Here and Now experience—ranging anywhere from a simple sense of well-being to the heightened state of ecstasy. Meditation's "mindfulness" practice ushers us to these golden thresholds like little else can. Remember, when you re-member, you consciously and deliberately re-join the All from which you are, were, and always will be inseparable. Without this recognition, you have but a limited, involuntary use of that connection. Sure, your heart will continue to beat, but it will not fly. And yes, you probably will survive, but you will not thrive.

When mindfulness is accomplished, you create for yourself the epitome of a clean slate. In Thought Farming parlance, you are a "ready field," and as exceptional and as inviting as this prospect may now seem, initially most people run screaming from this heightened level of moment-by-moment awareness and unfettered "beingness." As a child, you may have gotten burned at the hot oven of your parents' boiling rage. Or maybe it was the icy chill of their cold "distance"—emotional abandonment stings just as much. In either case, you are not likely to welcome a direct encounter with the Here and Now, be it in relation to a parent, the world, or even to yourself, without some new assurances.

-29- | When You Reach the End Of Your Rope, Let Go!

Guarantees are a big selling point in any business. Give me a guarantee and I'm considerably closer to making any new investment. I'd imagine you are a lot like me in that respect. Well, you are in the process of selling yourself on a great many new ideas and possibly a whole new way of approaching life. My guess is that you are going to be hoping for some kind of a warranty. Heck, you wouldn't even buy a new refrigerator without one.

But guarantees, as comforting as they are, are only about as good as the paper they're printed on. If the company issuing that guarantee goes belly-up, that piece of paper becomes good kindling at best. So, there must be something else going on, something that gets silently thrown into the deal each time you take a new risk, even when there is a guarantee attached to it. That quiet "something," that silent partner in all your affairs— business and personal—is what is known as Faith. You have faith, for instance, that Sears is going to be around tomorrow should your ice cubes melt. Why? "Well," you say to yourself, "They've been around forever. It's a good bet." You want to make very sure that the "company" with which you do your psychological, emotional, and spiritual business is at least as sound as Sears.

~~~

Ultimately, to experience true happiness, you are going to need to "let go," to trust Life itself, the "company" with which you are, after all, doing *all* your business. It is in the process of "letting go," of victoriously surrendering into Life, that you are relaxed enough to finally experience your previously lost sense of well-being. Relaxing proves prerequisite, both to the alpha and the omega of enlightenment. You are, by "letting go," quite literally "lighter," having jettisoned all your old reasons for holding on in the first place.

Ironic as it may be, and for what you assumed was your own safety, you have held tight to your limiting beliefs, thinking somehow that there was greater safety in "knowing"—good or bad—valuing familiarity more highly than possibility. This need to know, for judging, for comparing, for labels and definitions, is something you will want to relinquish. Joy is an experience. Thought disrupts experience. Thought must be relaxed.

To accomplish this, you could take each item on your "What negative judgments do I make about myself?" list, one at a time, and challenge and refute each one. This is the essence of *The Truth and the Lie Game*, and it is a good solid tool to have and use for the incidental rogue belief. But why mess with a hoe when you have a tractor sitting in the barn? If you want to put your "clearing" process into high gear, "letting go" is the way to go.

I am speaking, of course, of a psychological and an emotional "letting go" . . . regardless of what happened to you in your past. Whether you were abandoned, abuse, or neglected—if you could simply let it go it would be as good as gone. I wish that by saying this I would be implying that it is easier in some way. Unfortunately, this is not the case. That is why *The Truth and the Lie Game* proves so handy in the early stages. Our mind's grip on life is typically vise-like. Our old beliefs die hard. To borrow from Dylan Thomas, they do indeed rage, rage against the dying of the light. They do *not* go gentle into that good night. But as tough as "letting go" is, it is doable. With deliberate and continued effort, I guarantee it.

To begin, I have found that visuals help a great deal in the "letting go" process, so I will give you the one that finally worked for me. I pondered the nature of "letting go" for a very long time. I knew that there was something to it that could serve me in some dramatically beneficial way (like releasing the lion's share of my viscous self-judgment), yet I was scared to death to even consider it. Who would I be? If I slipped into a state of pure, unencumbered awareness, would I still be me? How would I know myself without my precious beliefs and feelings to give me quality?

I began very slowly by first allowing myself representations, looking for a virtual experience of "letting go." I found it brilliantly symbolized within the scary world of daredevil antics. The stunt that stood out in my mind the most vividly—the sensation I imagined coming closest to the fearsome notion of "letting go," was skydiving—*sans* parachute. So, here we go . . .

~ ~ ~

Every night for weeks, as I prepare to fall asleep, I fantasize that I jump out of an airplane *so high* that I can never, ever see the ground. This works like a charm, in that it immediately summons the very same anxiety/terror I feel when contemplating the idea of psychologically "letting go." My apprehension related to both the imaginary and the psychological release, I discover, is my fear of going "splat," of smashing up against some unknown, unseen obstruction somewhere "down there" that will annihilate me. It would probably be the ground in my fantasy, but who knew what psychologically?

So, in my imagination, I build a gigantic net that will follow me down as I fall. The net thing doesn't work too well, because it is awkward to imagine. Who, after all, is holding the net? This gives me another idea. God's hands could protect me as I fall. They could precede me, making sure that I'd be safe. That fantasy works . . . for awhile.

So then, every night, *this* would be my fantasy . . . Me leaping out of an airplane at some ridiculous height, with God's hands cupped beneath me, "sheltering" me, endlessly down. . . down. . . down. Ridiculous, right? But my anxiety begins to lessen bit by bit, and I can more calmly begin to entertain the notion of a psychological/emotional release. Was I on the verge, at long last, of relaxing my mind's analytical chokehold on my life?

Unfortunately, my relationship with God, Whoever or Whatever that is, is not yet firm enough to totally quell my fears—close, but no cigar. I need to take my fantasy one step further. What finally works is when I realize that my anxiety is based on the belief that there has to be a bottom to the fall. But there never *is* a bottom to the fall—never any ground at all upon which I ever go "splat." In my fantasy, I can easily accommodate for this, and when I plug "no ground" in, I immediately begin to relax. This has an incredibly positive effect, both on my feelings during the fantasy and on the analogous psychological "letting go" that I am ever-so-gingerly beginning to attempt.

Of course, I can let go. I can clearly see now how there is literally no downside to it. Even death, though a certainty, is surmountable—for indeed, even the finality of this is in question. No matter. I have taken back my freedom to fly.

~~~

Night after night, in my fantasies, fly I would. No fear, no anxiety—just pure exhilaration. I begin to incorporate that "letting go" feeling into my life; trusting one moment . . . and then another . . . and then another . . . and then . . . no "splat." Wow!

Then, at last, the revelation. All my fearful thinking, all those items on my "What negative judgments do I make about myself?" list *were* the rocks—the broken shards, the hard "truth" that I thought I'd surely smash into *if I gave up control*. People would unquestionably see how lazy, unintelligent, confused, scared, gullible, naive, vain, or whatever it was I thought I was. But just as there was no ground to crash into in my fantasy, there was no hard truth to collide with either. Giving myself permission to let go of all those old harmful ideas was the biggest gift I had ever given myself. I could, after years of self-abuse, finally relax. I could stop pretending not to be all those terrible things I never *actually* was in the first place. Again, no "splat." Wow!

My "elephant" was beginning to show.

~~~

Life works in mysterious ways. While assembling material for *When You Reach The End Of Your Rope, Let Go!*, I came upon the following:

"And if . . . transpersonal growth is engaged with great intensity, then at some point you will climb not just up the ladder, but off it. As Zen would say, you're at the top of a hundred-foot pole, and yet you must take one more step. How do you step off a hundred-foot pole? You take that step, and where are you? When you step off the ladder altogether, you are in free fall in Emptiness. Inside and outside, subject and object, lose all ultimate meaning. You are no longer 'in here' looking at the world 'out there.' The universe of One Taste announces itself, bright and obvious, radiant and clear, with nothing outside, nothing inside, an unending gesture of great perfection, spontaneously accomplished."[9]

—Ken Wilbur, *A Brief History Of Everything*

And this . . .

> **"Parachute, Longest Fall Without Parachute.**
> The greatest altitude from which anyone has bailed
> out without a parachute and *survived* (my italics) is
> 21,980 feet. This occurred in January 1942, when Lt.
> (now Lt. Col.) I.M. Chisov (USSR) fell from an
> Ilyushin 4 which had been severely damaged. He
> struck the ground a glancing blow on the edge of a
> snow-covered ravine and slid to the bottom. The
> human body reaches 99 percent of its low-level
> terminal velocity after falling 1,880 feet. This is
> 117–125 m.p.h. at normal atmospheric pressure in a
> random posture, but up to 185 m.p.h. in a head-down
> position."
>
> —*The Guinness Book of Records*

And this . . . .

> "Like the falling sky diver, we could check our
> state of existence at any instant during the descent
> and say happily, 'So far, so good!' The thrill . . . is
> due to the fact that you are experiencing in your body
> one of the most profoundly important philosophical
> realities of human existence. Having leapt, you find
> the universe sustains you. There is a story about
> Albert Einstein's view of human existence. Asked to
> pose the most vital question facing humanity, he
> replied, 'Is the universe friendly?' It's possible that
> the universe knows what it's doing and means you
> no harm. If you merely consider that possibility, and
> keep it in mind, you create a space for it to be realized
> in your conscious life experience. You might be
> surprised to discover that you actually inhabit a
> friendly universe."[10]
>
> —Dr. Irving Oyle, *The New Medicine Show*

And this . . . .

> In *Flow*, Mihaly Csikszentmihalyi tells of an
> experience that a friend of his had while in the Air
> Force. The friend recounted a gruesome story of a
> routine parachute training. While preparing for a
> drop, it was discovered that there weren't enough
> right-handed parachutes to go around, so one right-
> handed man was issued a left-handed chute. He was
> told that the parachute was identical to the others
> with the exception that the ripcord was on the left
> side of the harness. To make a long story short, all
> chutes opened save one. "There had been nothing
> wrong with the parachute. The problem had been that,
> while falling through that awful eternity, the man had
> become fixated on the idea that to open the chute he
> had to find the release in the accustomed place. His
> fear was so intense that it blinded him to the fact that
> safety was literally at his fingertips."[11]

We must let go of our limiting expectations, too, because our
safety, our joy, our evolution, indeed our very lives may depend
upon our accepting new possibilities. If we keep habitually
reaching for our "rip cords" in the same old places, we may one
day find ourselves plummeting to disaster when we could just as
easily be floating through life. A good new idea can salvage any
ritually negative experience. *Vis-à-vis* letting go, in *A Return To
Love*, author Marianne Williamson writes, "Surrender is not
weakness or loss. It is a powerful nonresistance. Through
openness and receptivity on the part of human consciousness,
spirit is allowed to infuse our lives, to give them meaning
and direction."[12]

I struggled for years to arrive at the above insights. And it
was only then, after finally achieving free-fall, that the universe
chose to grace me with these other beautiful skydivers.

-30- | Dancing with Myself

O.k., so the universe, or at least my portion of it, begins to look like it might not be such a hostile place after all. But what of its inhabitants? I soon remember that I am in a world filled with others. My fantasy has helped me to let go, to feel better about and safer within myself, but what about these others? Where do they fit into this newly earned trust? What can I do with my fears, my pain, and my expectations that relate to them?

In his book, *Cutting Loose: An Adult's "Guide To Coming To Terms With Your Parents*, Howard M. Halpern, Ph.D., says:
:

> "So the wounds of unloving, originally inflicted through no fault of your own, are there. Where can you begin the repair job? You can begin, first of all, by not constantly rubbing and reopening the wound through self-destructive songs and dances. Your need for loving is real, but if you take as your task trying to get your unloving parent or other unloving people to love you, you will end up confirming your 'unlovability.' Your need for loving is as real as a powerful thirst on a hot day, but if you were unbearably thirsty you would reach for a glass of cool water, not a glass of hot sand which you hoped you could convert into cool water. The needed task, then, is to reach for love *where it is available* (my italics) rather than to try to get it from someone from whom it is unattainable."[13]

Aha! There seems to be a choice here that I have not yet considered. Get love from where it can be gotten . . . or go without love. It would also appear that this part of the process, like the "letting go" exercise, must include a good deal of self-trust and attention. For sooner or later, we come to realize that we are the only ones to whom we can realistically and *routinely* turn for what we missed in childhood. Lovers and friends might be counted on for their support, but they cannot fill the great gaps created by our less than "good enough" upbringing. In fact, we probably picked our partner (or ex-partner) *because* of their similarity to an offending parent, so we can't count on them for much more than a heightened awareness of the issue. This fact makes it even more imperative than ever that we do what we can for ourselves.

To risk another overly trodden phrase; life is a dance—one hundred percent of the time. And though God may be supplying the music, we can either choose to sit this one out or join in. Partners may bring us great joy, but if we are to truly get what life has to offer, we need to enjoy the dance we do with ourselves.

~~~

It will be up to you to treat yourself in ways that you always wished you had been treated. Your tendency, however, will be to repeat the mistakes your parents made. Know this up front and watch for it. As much as you may desire a loving relationship with yourself, you will probably not be very comfortable with one. Loving gestures such as the type you will want to offer yourself will likely feel awkward and "undeserved."

Start doing little things for yourself every day. Buy yourself a small gift as a token of your self-love. Smile at a stranger. Follow through on a promise you made to yourself but never kept. Compliment yourself in the morning mirror. Take yourself out to dinner. These small acts of self-kindness will help you to "break the ice" that you long ago formed around your heart as an early act of self-protection.

> "Only what you have not given can be lacking from any situation."
>
> —*A Course in Miracles*

If you find that you are resistant to "giving," or are in some way uncomfortable even with the idea of it, search yourself for the reasons, and examine them as objectively as you can. Run them through *The Truth and the Lie Game* and The Emotional Detoxx. Work toward a "global release" by creating your own "letting go" fantasy, or try using mine. Your new, kinder behavior towards yourself and others is sure to summon from the shadows of your psyche many of the beliefs that have secretly stood in the way of your personal happiness.

It doesn't have to be much, but it is an evolutionary imperative: Begin in any way that you can, to be the best mother, father, sister, brother, friend, or lover you ever (or never) had.

Mystic Secret 6: *Your lasting security, your enduring sense of peace, joy, and well-being lies with the most valuable, most precious possession you own—that one thing most intrinsic— the only thing that belongs to you that can never be taken from you . . . **You**.*

Exercise 6: Recount as many things from your life that, at the time, you thought you absolutely just had to have. This could include cars, jobs, homes, jewelry, clothing, vacations, musical instruments, boyfriends, girlfriends, husbands, wives, children, etc.

List these separately on a clean sheet of paper. Under each, create two columns. In one column, write all the ways your life was improved by acquiring that item, person, or position. In the other column, list all the ways in which your life was negatively affected. This may be a painful exercise for some. No one but you will ever have to see the results of this personal accounting. No one but you could benefit as greatly from its conclusions.

For Example: Children

Positive	Negative
Unconditional love	No time for myself
Sense of purpose	Enormous responsibility
Greater joy	Diminished sex life
Learned how to give	No extra money
Ecstatic moments	Always afraid for their safety

In this exercise, you are not necessarily looking to undo or change anything. If through newfound awareness you find that you can make adjustments, then so much the better. Here, specifically, you are seeking both a heightened sense of yourself and of the results that come from personal choice. A more subtle awareness will be created from taking an honest inventory of the decisions that you have made. You may find that many of the things that you thought you simply couldn't live without have proven far less critical to the overall quality of your life than you originally suspected. This, in turn, may help you reprioritize, and be more levelheaded about your choices in the future.

-31- | C.

C. is a street-wise woman. And though full of life, she is also full of fear. She came to the United States with her mother from their native Mexico when she was nine, fleeing what C. would later describe as "a father prone to drink and rage."

C. married a man she knew she did not love. The day of the wedding, she confided in her best friend that she knew this marriage was a big mistake, but for some powerful, unknown reason, C. was unable to stop it. The marriage was a catastrophe. C. would not let her husband touch her for weeks, and when she finally did, her body barely responded—she was nearly frigid.

When provoked or frightened (she was easily both), C. would slip into an altered consciousness where she would lash out in fits of rage. Later C. would have no recollection of these episodes, but the bruises on her husband told of a woman out of control.

In addition to her marriage difficulties, C. was having trouble at work. She was a diligent, hard worker, yet her boss was constantly finding fault with her. C. related that she experienced a good deal of prejudice at the office, due to her Latin American origins. Life was miserable for this woman. Anxious and depressed, she became unable to meet her professional responsibilities. C. was soon "let go."

About the same time as her dismissal, C. found that she could no longer tolerate her loveless marriage, and she left her husband of less than a year. Her life quickly spiraled downward. She felt more and more a victim. Two years on, she was nearly suicidal.

That was when I first met C.

The day she entered my office, C. appeared extremely agitated. Her face and hands were sweaty, and she spoke a-mile-a-minute. Her voice was high-pitched and seemed slightly disconnected from the rest of her. Her dress was like that of any other twenty-something-ish young woman, but I soon realized that C. had the unfailing habit of carrying an extremely childish, cartoony sort of shoulder bag. Over the course of the next few sessions, I also noticed that C. wore boots that were fastened at the top with various Warner Brothers cartoon character lace-holders.

There was a look of fear and distrust on her face, and so I began our initial session by asking C. what she was so afraid of. C. could not answer me, though she voiced the suspicion that if she could, her healing would be well underway. The Emotional Detoxx work we began that day uncovered some powerful early memories . . . .

The origin of her oldest fear tested age three, so I asked if she had any recollections of that time period. C. recounted a horrifying episode that involved an argument between her parents one late night. The screaming was so intense that it had woken her, and when C. followed the loud voices into her parent's bedroom, she discovered her father violently beating her mother. When her father saw C. at the door, he momentarily stopped his attack, allowing her mother to break free and run from the house. This left C. alone with her enraged father . . . terrified. However, he then ran from the house in pursuit of his wife, carrying, as she recalled, a large kitchen knife.

C. wept deeply, reexperiencing the fear that had overwhelmed her that night so many years before. We explored the nature of her thoughts born from that terrifying incident (men are dangerous, I'm not safe, etc.), and she appeared to relax a bit.

~~~

In a subsequent session, we discovered feelings of abandonment, beginning age four. Asked if there were any memories that would support this discovery, C. vaguely recalled traveling through Mexico with her mother. At some point in their wanderings, C.'s mother needed to take work, which prevented her from caring for her daughter. C. was deposited in an orphanage, for what she later learned was nearly two months. Imprisoned in an institution, C. could not know when or if her mother would ever come back to reclaim her and to save her from what she could now only describe as "a living nightmare."

These memories became more and more vivid the further we explored C.'s past together. And with the help of The Emotional Detoxx, we were able to discern which current beliefs were born of her early mishandling. C. got worse before she got better. Raising these memories from the depths of her body/mind rendered her weak and slightly more depressed. But over time, C. began to distinguish herself from her thoughts and feelings. The more we delved the early conditions that spawned her most deeply held beliefs, the more she cried. And the more she cried, the more C. was able to release her body-conscious fears and feelings of abandonment.

~~~

There were now periodic "windows" of neutral, unencumbered beingness. And with these windows soon came hope. C. began to see that feeling other than terrified was a possibility. Over the course of our work together, she has stopped wearing her childish apparel. Her face and hands no longer sweat uncontrollably, and her speech has slowed to a normal cadence. Happy with herself at last, C. is now starting to desire men and, as of this writing, is dating successfully for the first time in her life.

-32- | Zoe, the Tiger, And the Dalai Lama

One day, around seven years ago, when my beautiful niece, Zoe, was just turning three, I took the liberty of asking her a most serious question. My logic was that here was a "being" relatively untainted by worldly woe, temporally as close to her creator as anyone I personally knew, and someone who possessed at least a modicum of verbal skills with which to communicate her insights. O.K., so I took a long shot.

We were sitting on the floor of Zoe's room playing some sort of made-up game with one of her picture puzzles. I turned to her, and with as much intent as one can summon when addressing a three-year-old child with a soggy cardboard puzzle-piece dangling from her lip, I asked, "Zoe, honey, what's the meaning of life? Why do you think we're here?" I know, I know—you probably think I'm nuts. But don't call the men in the white coats yet.

Zoe momentarily stopped her play, took the soggy cardboard out from between her tiny temporaries and, without missing a beat, matter-of-factly informed me, "To have fun, Uncle Geoffrey."

I was dumfounded, utterly shocked by her answer. Zoe's directness and the simplicity of her response temporarily masked the profundity of her message. I gave a bit of nervous laughter in response, feeling like the stereotypical perplexed goof, scratching his head.

But Zoe was quite serious, and her eyes spoke volumes as to her sincerity. As I recall it now, the next few moments felt like an epiphany. Here, as simple as simple could be, was Truth with a capital T—wisdom from the mouth of the newly verbal babe. I thanked Zoe for her answer and, with a kiss and a hug, told her that I thought she was absolutely right. I added that I would remind her of her early insight later in life if she ever forgot it. It was Jesus who said, "Except ye be as little children ye shall not enter into the Kingdom." This wisdom starts to look pretty undeniable. In retrospect, it seems self-evident that sharing Zoe's childlike intuitive belief in goodness and good times would go a long way toward reclaiming any lost sense of joy. Ah, but you say that you are an adult now, not a child anymore. Regardless, if you truly wish it, Thought Farming can help you grow this important quality back.

Joy is the natural result of direct experience—not all experience, but most—and so it will require you to establish a greater trust in and a deeper appreciation of yourself and your world. You cannot relax into that which you do not trust. We'll keep exploring the "how to" of this throughout these pages.

Permit me a quick personal note . . . Zoe is no ordinary run-of-the-mill niece. Oh sure, I'm a bit prejudiced like all loving uncles, but Zoe is the daughter of my identical twin brother, Sam. This means that she is genetically as much me as she is either her father or mother. Because of this, there is a uniqueness to our relationship—the kinship is palpable—the communication, clear and immediate. I somehow knew that I could count on her for an answer. I simply was not prepared for the one that I got.

Of course, I suppose it could be argued that Zoe's response was merely the natural result of her arguably limited perspective—the babbling of a naive young soul. After all, what does a three-year-old child know of responsibility, duty, or obligation? Surely, in coming to terms with life's necessities, the notion of having fun must finally be left buried in the toy chest, along with all the other fantasy playthings of youth . . . Or must it?

In an interview on the Oprah Winfrey show, Tiger Woods, golf's young superstar, had some interesting things to say *apropos* of the importance of fun. When Oprah asked him how it felt having been dubbed the sports world's Messiah by *GQ Magazine*, Woods' response ran through me like a jolt of electricity. He answered simply, "I'm just a human being like everyone else. I just want to have fun." Shades of soggy cardboard . . . I was immediately transported back to the floor of Zoe's room, as the dots began to do their mystical connecting dance in my brain.

When Oprah asked Woods' father, who also appeared on the show, for the secret to training the Tiger, he replied, "I kept everything a game, fun was the key." Now obviously Mr. and Mrs. Woods did a lot more for their young cub than just keep him laughing, but having fun was a crucial ingredient in the care and feeding of this formidable superstar.

Much of Woods' education, both on and off the golf course, proved remarkably successful. In response to Oprah's noting his grace, pleasant demeanor, and winning smile, Woods offered, "I'm just happy being Tiger Woods, and that's all there is to it. I was taught, and I believe, that anything is possible. I know of no boundaries inside myself."

Wow! No wonder Woods buried everyone at the 1997 PGA Masters Tournament, the 2000 U.S. Open, and continues to rule the sport as golf's number one ranked player. Such confidence! In awe-inspired resonance, Oprah's audience listens and applauds, as does Tiger's father, and I cry at the beauty of a father's recognition and celebration of his son.

~~~

If Zoe and Tiger haven't yet convinced you that you need to take fun more seriously, perhaps another voice on the subject might. In Mark Epstein's wonderful *Thoughts Without a Thinker*, The Dalai Lama, one of the world's great Thought Farmers, begins the Foreword: "The purpose of life is to be happy. As a Buddhist I have found that one's own mental attitude is the most influential factor in working toward that goal. In order to change conditions outside ourselves, whether they concern the environment or relations with others, we must first change within ourselves. Inner peace is the key. In that state of mind you can face difficulties with calm and reason, while keeping your inner happiness."[14]

This is the solid foundation, the very working explanation of a well-run Thought Farm. It may seem elementary, but if you incorporate this deceptively simple-sounding philosophy into your life and begin to move into activity inspired by its truly profound perspective, you will begin to see some remarkable results, almost immediately.

One of your chores as a Thought Farmer, then, will be to learn to develop and maintain this inner posture for yourself. Meditation, The Emotional Detoxx, and learning to let go and trust life, in tandem, work magic toward this end.

-33- | It's FUNdamental

In the course of my own evolution, as well as in the work that I do with clients, I have discovered the indisputable, profoundly workable truth virtually shouting from Zoe's, Tiger's, and the Dalai Lama's mutual philosophy. Fun plays the key role in living a rich, fulfilling life. It is the essence of all good feeling, the prerequisite as well as the by-product of all genuine acts of loving. Fun is the alpha and the omega of joy, its deeper, more profound emotional cousin.

But you say that you are not three years old anymore, you were not as fortunate as Tiger Woods in the parent department, and you cannot find it within yourself to give away all your worldly possessions to go live on a mountaintop in Tibet. What chance have *you* got to put more joy into your seemingly mundane life?

Thought Farmers (that includes *you*) are inherently fun-loving folks—people of wit and wonder. Many of us, though, have lost our senses of humor and adventure to the demands and complexities of our judgmental thinking. So seemingly hidden are the "lighter" life aspects, that we now routinely turn to spiritual leaders, political leaders, psychotherapists, financial wizards—gurus of all shapes and sizes—consulting any and every outside "authority" imaginable, in hopes of getting a bead on that elusive *joie de vivre*.

We have lost our natural ability to have fun. We have forgotten the fun-damentals.

Why? Well, we have learned through rigorous socialization

that there is more serious business to attend to, starting with keeping mother and father happy. This near fatal misconception is largely the result of the bad rearing we received so long ago, back on the family "farm." The burden of responsibility we shouldered as children for preserving a buoyant family dynamic is almost universally accepted; needing, as it seemed, to fend off our terrifying fears of abandonment and subsequent demise.

The problem with this awful arrangement is that we are setting ourselves up for a lifetime of other-oriented concern, hoping to get our share of love through the back door—by way of reciprocity—at the expense and suppression of our natural selves. **Instead of growing our own crops, we learn how to beg for food at the doors of our relations.**

It is only much later in life, as we begin to feel the gnawing emptiness within us, as we sense the hollow, hungry heart that pounds in our chest, that we realize our personal foundations have been severely compromised.

We feel lost. Well, we *are* lost. Somewhere we have made a wrong turn, somewhere very early on, back before the age of maps and reason, back in the shadowy beginnings of our distant pasts, and we are scared.

~~~

Whether you currently feel as though you are equipped to handle the job or not, you and only you can make your life grow again. The sooner you can reclaim your personal authority—by means of a full-bodied, mindful, and soulfully clear understanding and appreciation of who you are (and who you are not)—the sooner you will shed the old unworkable systems that you imposed upon yourself early on, when in virtual choice-less circumstance, you relinquished You. This is the end of conformity for the sake of acceptance, at the expense of actual Selfhood. And, as with all good endings, through the mystical cycle of death and rebirth, you will begin again.

> "That ending and that new beginning face you with what Kierkegaard called 'the alarming possibility of being able.' And why is being able alarming? Because it means breaking with all the messages you grew up with that say, 'Don't,' 'You can't,' 'You're too little.' Being able means severing the vestigial ties that leash you to the past . . . knowing your ultimate aloneness, knowing your weaknesses and your strengths, daring to turn your wishes and your potentials toward untried risks. If that isn't alarming, what is?"[15]

Yes, absolutely. Where you are headed may shake you up a bit. But what good would it be, what shift could it provide if it didn't? Kierkegaard's "alarming possibility of being able" may indeed shock you, but in no time at all it becomes a rather pleasant shock, indeed—like jumping into a cool lake.

~ ~ ~

I recall a childhood riddle that went something like this . . . Question: "Why do we always find what we're looking for in the last place we look?" Answer: "Because once we've found it, we stop looking." As silly as this sounds, it is true; and it segues nicely into something more importantly true.

The experience and discovery of purpose, which we will now call "Joy," will elude you *so long as you are looking for it.* Sounds like a catch-22, doesn't it? But joy cannot be found through any search. Like Parsifal, the "Grail" will lie just beyond your reach, though you may search a lifetime.

Strange as it may seem, you will find meaning only after you've *stopped* looking for it. More precisely: A "searching" frame of mind, fueled by longing, breeds only more searching and greater longing. In contrast, a "discovery" mentality, fueled by acceptance, breeds greater discovery and enhanced experience. Pursue happiness, and it *will* elude you. Live "rightly," and happiness will happen to you. I know it seems like "You can't get there from here," but you can and you will.

One of life's great cosmic clues is that the words "happen" and "happiness" have the same etymological root. Living "rightly" is not complicated, but it does require you to have an open mind and a willingness to relinquish your old unworkable beliefs. It necessitates a basic trust in life and, consequently, a "let-go" of your efforts to control it or muscle it into submission. It also asks that you be adventurous, so that you are inclined to test for yourself the validity of what might initially appear to be frightening or unbelievable new ideas.

~~~

An analogy might help to clarify the important distinction between "searching" and "discovering." Learning to appreciate computerized 3-D artwork offers an interesting comparison. In order for you to "get the picture," you have to relax and *defocus*. You do not hunt, you *accept*. It is exactly the same when it comes to an ability to experience joy. If life feels too much like a joke that everyone is getting except you, maybe it's because you are trying too hard. After all, trying is not fun, it's . . . well, *trying*.

Another good analogy that might help you to get a feel for the curious power of "yielding" and "acceptance" is the Chinese "finger torture"—that multi-colored woven finger toy that can trap you within it. Once your fingers are inside, you can pull and pull, but to no avail—the more you pull, the tighter its grip. Your only hope is to relax, then gently push your hands *together*. In this way alone may you slip your fingers to freedom. This is beautifully analogous to the counter-intuitive approach to problem-solving and the creation of joy that we will continue to explore, and that all good Thought Farmers employ.

~ ~ ~

Much in the same way that the watched pot refuses to boil, neither will you "bubble" with any exuberance for life if you scrutinize its every moment. A good Thought Farmer knows he needn't perpetually watch his fields for his crops to grow. You, too, must learn to relax, secure in knowing that the elements are hard at work for you as well—once you have properly set them in motion.

Our journey together involves an exploration, explanation, and application of this and other obscure yet vital bits of Truth. There are many discoveries ahead on the road to letting go. And like the proverbial Arab who wanders off into the desert to seek the meaning of life (just to find upon his return that his "revelation" has no bearing back at the bazaar—the world of commerce and counter-agendas) you, too, must ultimately have answers that go deep enough so as to stand the test of real-life application.

-34- | Mood Control To Major Tom

Ever been in a funk? You drag yourself around for hours, days, even weeks sometimes, under your own personal storm cloud. Then, either swept away by time or a turn of events, your mood shifts, the sun comes out, and your heart feels light again. Ever wonder, "What the heck is going on with me?" Quite often, anxiety/depression proves the culprit—negatively charged energy that seems to "come out of nowhere." You're going through your day on a fairly even keel, when all of a sudden your mood takes a downward turn for the worse. Like a pilot who can't pull his plane out of a death-spiral, you begin to plummet . . . .

You are much too heavy. You are going down!

Anxiety attacks can be extremely disruptive, and they may involve feelings of great fear or panic. *Analyze This*, the 1999 Billy Crystal/Robert DeNiro film, depicts these nonentertaining episodes rather entertainingly since it's the mob boss who is having them.

Having no immediately identifiable cause, anxiety is often referred to by the term "free floating." Free floating . . . . It sounds so lovely, doesn't it? This is a bit of a misnomer, however. Anxiety comes at a rather high price, and there is nothing "floating" about it.

After working with many anxious clients, I've come to believe anxiety's hidden cause to be generally one of two things. It is either a reaction to an individual or to an event that carries some negative associative weight, subconsciously retriggering an earlier upset; or even more subversively, it is a response to a basic "lack" we perceive in ourselves—a feeling of worthlessness, groundlessness, or unlovability that quickens periodically, undermining us at our core. So pervasive and unsettling is this perception that it often colors our whole life in unflattering, unsettling shades, producing within us everything from a general malaise, or "blah" feeling, to, in a worst case scenario, sheer terror.

~~~

For starters, you will want to understand that, unlike fear, anxiety's cause is internal—it is within you. The "danger" is neither clear nor imminent. Therefore, standing up to the anxiety, weathering it, will usually send it packing. As painful as these feelings can be, you will actually want to welcome them in. Whenever I begin to feel anxious, I literally say to myself, "O.K., show me everything you've got. I'm not afraid of you." Sounds a bit silly, I know, but it works. Within seconds, the anxiety is relieved.

The Truth and the Lie Game comes in pretty handy here, too. Once the tremulous event is under control, taking stock of what "really is" can help to further secure the calm. These techniques are good stop-gap measures on the way to a deeper understanding of yourself, but it is imperative that you continue to explore your beliefs and feelings wherever they appear to be getting in the way of what you want or how you want to feel. Until they are recognized and renegotiated, these nonbeneficial beliefs and feelings are impediments.

~~~

Some repressed definition of yourself, some judgmental belief/label you slapped on yourself and promptly began resisting years ago, is undoubtedly the cause of your inner turmoil. By discovering it, welcoming it back in, and allowing yourself to feel whatever there is to feel about it (as opposed to repressing or denying your feelings), you will be giving the old resisted energy new voice within you. The more that you do this, the safer you will feel giving your previously repressed hurt feelings "air time." The more voice that you give these hitherto split-off, disenfranchised parts of yourself, the more "whole," the more "You," you will begin to feel. Over time, there will be less and less opportunity for anxiety to get a foothold within you, and more and more opportunity for happiness to happen.

~~~

"Disenfranchisement" is at the center of much of our emotional upset and neurosis. What happens is, as a young child, you make certain decisions about various aspects of yourself, choosing some as acceptable and others as not. That which is deemed unacceptable is done so, typically, in reaction to a parent or significant other that seems to have withdrawn their love or support for you in response to a particular behavior or personal aspect.

If as a child, for instance, every time I get excited my voice raises in pitch and I become overly animated, bothering mother or father to the point that they yell at me to calm down, I may get the idea that they no longer love me when I get excited about something. If this reaction is severe enough and repeated with sufficient frequency, I will probably "split off" from my excitability, as its price has now become too high.

When this occurs, I no longer have an avenue for the natural expression of my enthusiasm, having blocked it in hopes of greater acceptance. Later in life, when I'm scratching my head wondering why I get anxious at times other people seem to be getting excited, it will behoove me to welcome that anxiety in, full force, thereby enabling me to reestablish a connection to my lost excitability. I will need to brave the currently illogical trembling I now face in order to allow my split-off enthusiasm readmittance. I will not feel complete until I do.

Mystic Secret 7: Forgotten emotion is the mortar that holds your inner walls together—the energetic stuff of your "I can'ts" and "Why bothers?" When you remember the emotion, the mortar dissolves and the walls come-a-tumbling down.

Before you can fully reengage the evolutionary process, you have to come "home," you have to return to wholeness. The road back to the essential You is strewn with emotions—feelings and personal aspects which you systematically abandoned as a child, but which actually remain hidden within you, unexpressed. *Don't blame yourself for this.* These emotions were probably suppressed because they were just too big to handle at the time you first began to feel them.

Exercise 7: Make a list of all the ways you are critical of yourself and others—the judgments you routinely make. This, and your Exercise 2 list, will probably have many elements in common. That's O.K. You will want to take a particularly close look at those beliefs that appear on both lists.

Examining your beliefs will help you uncover feelings you may have forgotten you still have. Please do not prejudge this exercise, even if you have had years of psychotherapy. I can assure you, if that therapy consisted solely of "talking heads," you will be in for some interesting surprises.

By doing Exercise 1, that is, by repeating, *"I am now aware of my limiting beliefs,"* you are giving consent to your subconscious mind to release information up into your consciousness. Consent, as you shall see, is a crucial ingredient, virtually dictating what you will and will not allow into your experience. Keep your list of judgments, complaints, and criticisms handy and active. Carry it with you. This is an exercise-in-progress. Do not try to come up with all your negative beliefs in just one sitting. In that manner, you will omit more than you will recall.

Remind yourself that you are becoming more and more aware of your limiting thought and talk. Keep Exercise 1 going. Though it may seem unpleasant to tune your awareness into what you might consider the dark side of your personality, it will soon serve a most enlightening purpose.

Successful Thought Farming, like its agricultural namesake, requires that you follow certain steps. You are, by unearthing your limiting beliefs, essentially clearing the land—weeding the garden. You *cannot* skip this part. Muscle test each belief to make sure that it is, indeed, one of yours, and not simply a hunch. Phrase your beliefs in slightly different ways, testing each individually. Some words will trigger associations while others may not. For instance, "Sex is dirty" may test "yes", whereas "sex is bad" may test "no."

Follow The Emotional Detoxx self-testing outline on pages 95 through 97. Remember, you are in the process of a great liberation . . . a consciousness revolution/evolution.

If it makes you feel any better, keep in mind that, as with flower or vegetable gardening, the initial ground preparation is hardest. The planting and the harvest are much more enjoyable.

-35- | J.

J. is a bright, handsome, talented man. He is married to a beautiful woman who obviously adores him, and by all accounts, J. should be a very happy guy. But J. is not . . . and he cannot understand what is "wrong" with him.

J. grew up, as I was to learn, a little too fast. His mother inappropriately relied on him in many "adult" ways. Far too early on, she sought J.'s advice as well as his company. His father, on the other hand, was competitive with him. He would challenge J. to all sorts of games of skill and strategy and then would gloat if he would win.

Despite this treatment, J. believed that whatever he set his mind to he could accomplish. The problem was in how J. felt; he was never satisfied. J. was always thinking that there was something else he could or should have done; somewhere he could have improved upon himself or his performance.

By making, then testing the statement "I'm enough," and getting a "no" answer, J. began his Emotional Detoxx.

Though, historically, he had successfully met most of his challenges, J.'s "body-consciousness" held that he was, as this man put it, "ineffectual." When asked to be overly responsible too early in life, many people succumb to the painful belief that they are insufficient in some way. They do not have the where-withal to realize that what they are being asked to do is beyond the scope of *anyone* their age. They incorrectly assume that there is something wrong with *them*. This all-too-painful thought/feeling then gets buried deep within their body/mind.

Ironically, they will then go about asserting the very opposite (as a know-it-all does for his sense of inadequacy) in an attempt to compensate for what was simply too painful a "truth" to admit to themselves.

Using The Emotional Detoxx, J. began uncovering a host of nonbeneficial feelings and beliefs that he had carried practically his whole life. These feelings related to J.'s mother and her inappropriate demands on him, and to his father and his need to put J. down. The stage was set for J.'s assumption that he was never quite good enough.

~~~

There was something else working on J., though. He had been raised a Christian, with a deep respect for and fear of God. As J. grew into a more independent thinker, he could not reconcile his growing belief in Union and the Oneness of everything with his early and entrenched belief that God was *outside* of himself, judging his every thought and deed.

J. was a man now separate from his God, separate from himself. Finding no solace in the church, he could no longer accept the old version of things. But horrible guilt plagued him if he tried believing otherwise. All of this "stuff" came up and out of him very quickly in the work we did together. When these "truths" were finally revealed—through muscle testing—and ushered back into his consciousness, J. was able to renegotiate with himself and to accept a new "story" as to what God meant to him now and who he seemed to be in relation to God.

Without images in his head of a judgmental God Who he would have to appease, a mother who he would have to please, and a father who would deal unfairly with him, J. began to relax. He is not nearly so hard on himself anymore. And though just as capable as ever, the big difference now is that J. is much kinder to himself and far more capable of finding joy in his achievements.

| Love

Love isn't something you find, it's something you *do*.

Tracey Woodward

A good rule of thumb is to remember that any attributes that you routinely look for in your partners represent aspects of yourself that lie un- or underdeveloped. If, for instance, you want a "strong" mate, you must work toward strengthening yourself. If you tend toward highly generous people, you must allow yourself more generosity. If you seek the fun loving, you need learn how to create more fun for yourself. If you tend to attract strong-willed partners, you'll want to strengthen your own resolve. If you look for highly emotional companions, freeing-up your own emotions will be a priority.

In his best-selling book, *Getting The Love You Want, A Guide For Couples*, Harville Hendrix, Ph.D., says, " . . . in marriage the impulse to unite with the partner is unconsciously an attempt to reunite with the split-off parts of the self, which are projected onto the partner."[16]

True, but looking for completion in that one special "someone" has gone from national pastime to national disaster. Vicarious strength withers quickly—the divorce rate is over fifty percent these days. Disenfranchisement is also at the root of what might best be called our "existential pain"— the feeling of isolation and aloneness. This all-to-common experience is characterized by a lack of a basic sense of well-being, of "completeness." Much to our dismay (and contrary to popular myth), the hunger for "wholeness" can never be satisfied by another.

I used to hate Walt Disney, for he always made finding love/joy in the face of that perfect "other" look so easy, so simple, so desireable. There's Cinderella and *her* prince. Snow White and *her* prince. Even Belle got into the act by finding love with her "Beast," who, if memory serves, also turned out to be a prince. All of Disney's heroines found their perfect love, all ending up with princes. I used to *hate* Walt Disney.

Then one morning while I was performing my shower version of "Whistle While You Work," I had nothing short of a revelation. These cartoon heroines were no ordinary girls. Each had a tremendous capacity for life and love; each was depicted as constantly communing with all sorts of wildlife, singing merrily to anything or anyone that would listen—loving . . . *loving.*

That was *it.* That was the real magic in each of these fairy tales. It's no wonder that Cinderella, Snow White, and Belle got what they incessantly sang about—they embodied these qualities *within* themselves. Each had such marvelous *inner* life. Each radiated love that was palpable, love that was unconditional. It was only a matter of time before the Law of Correspondence would work its "magic" and provide each with her prince. Walt, I apologize. Whether you knew it or not, you had it right all along.

Cinderella, Snow White, and Belle needn't be your role models. But you do need to get their stories straight before you write them off as mere fictional characters. If you are to create what *you* dream of in this life, you, too, must embody the dream-like corresponding characteristics and not hope for completion within relationship.

You were "whole," though not fully developed, at some point in your life—usually, as Buber said, for about a split-second right around the moment of birth. Then you began to shed various personal aspects—one by one—as push came to shove, and the "wicked witches" of your world began scaring you into submission. There are definite steps you can take toward "wholeness," even if you currently find yourself living co-dependently or hero-izing others, in response to your diminished sense of yourself.

The fact of the matter is, your heroes are your heroes and your lovers are your lovers because they embody aspects of your own that lie dormant. You are drawn to them from a place of harmonic resonance. If you had already "filled out" in these areas, you would be creating your own rich harmonic structure, without the need of their energy. So as you grow, you may still admire and respect these individuals, but hero worship will eventually be a thing of the past.

For example, one client who I will call P., had tremendous difficulty in claiming her personal authority. This prevented her from dealing with her bad marriage, and it inhibited her from using her great mind to further her career in medicine. Her best friend happened to be a very confident woman who constantly yet unsuccessfully tried to bolster P.'s self-esteem. In working with P., it quickly became apparent that she had been raised with some extremely damaging beliefs regarding the worth, or more accurately, the worthlessness of women in general. Both her grandfather and father's message to her was that she would need a man to get by, and that she ought not seem too intelligent, lest she ruin her chances of "catching a good one."

P.'s best friend, it turned out, was also her hero, and P. tried over and over again to emulate her. But the messages from her past haunted P., keeping her trapped—at the mercy of every man in her life—including her teenage son. It became clear to me that P.'s "pedestalizing" of her friend was all about her own inability to challenge the limits imposed upon her early on, and her frustration with not being able to access the personal strengths and abilities that lay dormant within her.

Helping P. to understand the nature of her hero worship, helping her to see that she was simply responding to aspects that she already possessed, gave her the solid ground upon which she needed to stand in order to challenge her old prejudicial messages. She could then begin to champion herself, backed by the support of the hero *within* her.

~~~

Our choice of lovers and mates often contains within it some component of hero worship. If, as it is with our heroes, we are routinely attracted to similar strengths in our choice of partners, it is practically a sure bet that the qualities we find so appealing in these "special" others, are personal aspects of ours that are sorely in need of development.

All this may not entirely be news to you, but there is something you might not know that could help you do something about it. *You seek these qualities in your lovers for the sake of balance and wholeness.* Remember, your heroes have been your heroes because they have energetically gone where you want to go. You cherish them from a place of what feels to be an inner emptiness. If you can fill this "hole" you have left in your soul, you eliminate the need to seek vicarious completion through others.

Essentially, your heroes and the other romanticized people in your life, simply represent yet another misguided step toward health. But loving in the name of need, in an ironic, twisted, mirror-image sort of way, makes about as much sense as killing in the name of God. In each case, you end up destroying any chance of personalizing and integrating the very qualities you fly as your colors and claim as your cause.

In our romantic conquests, we temporarily trick ourselves into feeling complete, then invariably find that we must pay the piper, usually in heaps of emotional currency—typically tithing for years with our dependency issues and the inevitable fear of abandonment. It just doesn't work; never has, never will. Your "crusades," therefore, must be inner journeys, and not outward searches, if they are ever to yield satisfying, lasting results.

Your only hope for ongoing happiness, a sense of well-being, inner confidence, and personal autonomy is reparation of yourself. You must retrieve all those jettisoned personal aspects that you, in Hansel and Gretel fashion, have left scattered behind you on your wayward wanderings from "home." Then you may know personally, *first-hand*, your hitherto lost sense of wholeness. Then, too, may you finally stop looking in the places and the faces of others for what is irreplaceably your own.

Most of us aspire to the "idea" of love. We dream of it, reach for it, hope for it, and pray for it. We look for it out there as if it were discoverable through some sort of archaeological dig. Well, dig this: You cannot know any love that is not your own . . . ever. If someone told you that they loved you, you would just have to take their word for it, wouldn't you? I mean, how could you be sure? How would you know the depth of that love, the strength, or the resilience? You could not. You could never be inside of them to know for certain what they were feeling. All you can ever know is your own heart. But if love is what you desire, then that is all you will ever need know.

Love is given. Love is for giving. You cannot give what is not yours to give. If love is what you want, then you must give it. Love is its own reward.

Many of us have been on either side of an unrequited love. I have loved and not been loved back. And I have been loved when there was little in me that resonated with that lover. Neither is optimal, but, in my opinion, one is far more preferable. It is my experience that being loved when there is no mutuality to it proves a rather heavy, awkward experience. But me *doing* the loving—even when unrequited—ah! That is a vibrant experience. There is the intensity (painful though it may be). There is the exhilaration (crazy-making, though it certainly can get). There is the glow. And there is that mysterious "rush" that our songs, books, and movies unmercifully dangle before us, pumping through *my* very own veins.

So it seems that the benefit of love is found in the experience of it, generated inside yourself. Then, if you are additionally fortunate, you get to share the joy that that experience brings. No amount of *being* loved can come close to the magic of even one fleeting moment wherein you are the lover.

The trouble most of us run into occurs when we attribute our feelings of love to the love object (just another form of hero worship). If I love a flower, a sunset, a dog, a cat, or the wind on my face, these things may inspire my love, but it is still *my* love— to be spent the way I choose to spend it. I have learned that it is this capacity for love that mystically resides within me, with which I am most enamored. I cherish this life-enhancing aspect of myself, that I can feel so deeply about people, issues, and endeavors. When I own this remarkable quality, that which I love becomes secondary to my love *for* it. Yes, I would dearly miss certain people in my life should they suddenly vanish, but I know that it is my ability to love them that creates their immense value to me in the first place.

I have learned to love myself, in no small part, for the depth, the value, and the meaning I seem so able to impart to my world. Any aspect of that world is lovable, *should I choose to love it.* For instance, it is my choice whether I will ever love you. You may send me beautiful gifts, write me reams of inspired poetry, whisper sweet-nothings in my ear—but if my heart is cold, your efforts will entirely be in vain.

If, however, I *choose* to love you, you wouldn't even have to lift a finger. You see, my love for you is a gift that I give *myself.* If you happen to offer yourself the gift of a love for me, then perhaps you and I might choose to build a relationship based upon our mutual affections. Then, perhaps not. The more I love, the less each love object holds power over me, as I realize more and more whose energy fuels that love. I may wish to share my love with a number of different people, or perhaps I'd like to settle down and commit the lion's share of my love to you. What will help me make this choice will be an understanding and appreciation of my own loving nature.

As beauty is in the eye of the beholder, love is in the heart of the lover. If you wish to love, look no further than that which is directly in front of you. If you wish to be loved, look no further than yourself. In an ironic sort of way, it is only then—when you have succeeded in satisfying these preconditions—that you may draw to you a like-minded partner.

~ ~ ~

Now sex is another story altogether! More often than not, it precariously occupies the tip of our emotional icebergs. This typically makes it about everything *except* physical ecstasy or procreation, which are its natural functions.

True sexual fulfillment requires a healthy relationship with yourself and with the Here and Now. This relationship is exactly what this book is designed to help you create. Great sex will be a natural by-product of your doing your Emotional Detoxx work.

Sex isn't love and love isn't sex. A deeper appreciation of yourself will help you draw your own ethical and moral conclusions. However, to have both sex and love together in the same package is an extraordinary experience and worth striving for. If you presently feel as though you have sexual "issues," just keep doing your emotional clearing work. It may take some time to prove it to yourself, but I'll bet you dollars-to-donuts that you haven't got a "sexual" problem at all.

And once you've addressed the emotions underlying your thoughts, feelings, and behaviors, I'll bet you again that there will be nothing left to deal with . . . except, maybe, *other* people's hang-ups.

Mystic Secret 8: *What you love most about your lovers and heroes, you miss most about yourself.*

Exercise 8: When you find yourself perpetually drawn to the same type of men or women, decipher the code. What quality do they possess, or do you *think* they possess, that make them so appealing to you? Then, make as some of your most immediate goals, the development of these aspects within yourself. This is a simple way for you to know where your next bit of personal work may lie, without the need of any outside opinions or sophisticated analytical tools.

Make a running list of the qualities you are most attracted to in other people. It could look something like this:

—Honest, compassionate, courageous, spirited, generous, warm, confident, loving, spiritual, open-minded, adventurous, spontaneous, creative, good-natured, assertive, good-humored, active, attractive, worldly, etc., etc., etc.

When you've finished, save your list, and refer to it often. Any item on it that you don't yet personally own waits for you on the horizon of your evolutionary frontier.

-37- | You Are the Wind Beneath Your Wings

Retrieving ourselves, learning to love—both ourselves and others—and reaching the end of our ropes and finally letting go, typically require great courage and wisdom. Courage is needed to transcend our fears; wisdom helps us to transcend our beliefs. Sadly, there are no schools that can teach us how to do all of this. Our churches, synagogues, and childhood homes typically fall short as well. The reason for this seeming negligence is that, in order to teach these skills, one would need to have gained mastery oneself, and there are but a smattering of fully-nurtured, fully-integrated people running around. The few that there are probably couldn't begin to tell you how they got there themselves. These are not the experts; these are the fortunate ones.

Work of this nature has, by default, been left to the therapy session. There, we assume that we are in the presence of a master. In some cases we are. In others, we are not. Either way, it is imperative that we look upon rescue as *self*-rescue as early as possible. For, at best, the therapist serves only as a guide, helping us to avoid certain pitfalls along our recovery road, while mirroring us in ways that may help us to see ourselves more clearly.

If a therapist is very good, he or she has probably been through some growing pain and soul searching themselves, and will recognize the compensatory dances we unconsciously do. The therapist may offer their own war stories in an attempt to "universalize" what seems so overwhelmingly personal. This alone, if presented therapeutically, in the language of *our* pain, could save us years of trial-and-error searching.

~~~

Since our therapist is not caught up in the same old tangled tango as we and our family members are, he or she can usually help us unravel our old unworkable systems and facilitate our choosing new, more self-benefiting beliefs and behaviors.

But the bulk of the work—the inspiration and the momentum—all lie with *you*. Even in the face of extreme self-hate, you will need to find some reason to become your own best friend. Though your therapist may be your closest personal ally, creating for you a safety zone wherein you can begin to regain your trust, courage, and sense of yourself, it is you who must want to make your life feel and run better—you who must stick to that cause with fierce dedication.

Whether or not you have found yourself an effective therapist, you must understand that you manage your case, not them. As any good practitioner already knows: *You are the only true authority in your life*; not he or she, nor your mother or father, nor your husband or wife, nor your boss. No one knows what is best for you better than you do.

A search for personal joy that saddles itself with an outside standard must finally fail. Any guru worth his loincloth will tell you that you must ultimately leave him by the side of your evolutionary path. I tell my clients that the sooner they can divest me of any authority in their lives whatsoever, the better off they will be. Successful Thought Farmers are always, finally, self-made.

~~~

The task, then, is simple: Personally remove whatever obstacles lie between you and your ability to *be* you. Now if it were only as easy as it is simple! Well, here is the good news and the bad news: It is as easy as you let it be or as difficult as you make it. You will notice that the operative word here is *you*. No one can teach you how to *be* you. It is not that they don't care or that they are trying to be mean; they *can't* teach you because they don't know how. Only you are equipped with all the "you-ness" necessary for the job. You are the only *you* there is.

-38- K.

K. was, as I like to say, rather high up on the evolutionary ladder when I first met her. She was a happy, enthusiastic gal whose life was working in far more ways than most. There were, however, some rough spots. K. was an actor who dabbled as a landscaper and a physical trainer. Unable to understand why she wasn't landing much acting work, K. sought me out.

In one of our earliest sessions, K.'s body-consciousness revealed that she didn't actually want to *be* an actor at all. There were, we uncovered, far too many stereotypical connotations associated with actors in general for K.'s liking. As a result, she did not want to relate to herself as a member of that particular profession.

Once we uncovered this little glitch in her thinking/intention, it was easy to renegotiate that particular thought form. "Alright," I said, "if you don't want to *be* an actor—then be *you*, and just act." K. liked that idea, and she immediately began making changes. She got herself a new agent, changed her look, cut her hair, and got some new promotional photographs taken. Things were looking good—all the ducks seemed in a row—and I thought that K. was on her way.

But the jobs continued to elude her. There was, as we were to learn, more to K.'s dilemma than mere semantics.

Using The Emotional Detoxx tools, we soon discovered that K.'s intention was not to act theatrically at all, but rather to "behave grandly," to act out, to have the *lifestyle* of an actor. She sought to have a free-form daily regime. She wanted to exercise her many facets—as an actor might—to give play to her multiple energies, to give free reign to her complexity. K. also enjoyed the loosely structured nature of the actor's life—the fly-by-the-seat-of-the-pants, day-by-day approach to living.

When K. realized that she could create all this without having to "pretend" or follow someone else's script, she was euphoric. She immediately abandoned her interest in an acting career, concentrating instead on her work as a physical trainer. In that line of work, she was able to make her own schedule, while still enjoying the relative security of day-to-day sessions with clients. In this capacity, she was also able to draw on her many faceted persona, offering to clients just the right approach to training that worked best for them. Every day was just different enough and, more importantly, completely malleable by her.

K. never looked back. This woman had accomplished what she had actually intended to all along—K. had created her ideal lifestyle.

-39- | You Are Your Only Hope

I have said that creating the life you want entails, among other things, discovering, accepting, and ultimately letting go of your nonessential, nonbeneficial "self"—your non-elephant stuff. You might question the wisdom of this "letting go" in that it seems so drastic. But you are your only hope. *You*—not the applique. When you do "let go," you reach a level of awareness that transcends the invented separate-sense "self" and more and more approximates the authentic connected "Self." By incremental release of the small, belief-based "you," you naturally gain greater and greater access to the "larger," essential "You."

Additionally—and as a direct consequence of this victorious surrendering—life begins to be lived more experientially, non-judgmentally—you become truer and truer to your "Self." Mostly this will happen naturally, as you ease the grip that your analytical mind has had on you. The life you seek, regardless of your personal goals, requires this surrender—this experiential, moment-to-moment approach to living. Otherwise you are as a blind man before a sunset. You know that something beautiful is happening out there, but you cannot be sure exactly what it is— nor can you share in it.

~~~

As you search deeper and deeper through and for "you," you begin realizing all the things that you are not, because anything that can be witnessed is not the Witness itself. Any aspect of yours that can be examined, considered, scrutinized, and subsequently altered must, by its mutable nature, *not* be of the essential "you," or "You" in the larger sense.

It would seem to follow, then, that this "essential" you, this "Witness," if you will, must either be pure awareness and nothing else, or (now bear with me for a second) it is *everything* that is in that awareness, undifferentiated—simply taking turns in consciousness. In either case, the deeper one goes, the more one realizes that he is one Thing, either *nothing* or *everything*, but *one* Thing.

This is not mere philosophical babble. If it appears to be, I invite you to further plumb your personal depths. When you do, "I" will be there. I will be the one wearing the Cheshire cat smile. Reason being: There, at our mutual innermost, you and I merge, as, in the beautifully poetic imagery of Ken Wilber, we joyfully intersect the infinite. This stuff is important for you to know, now. Discovering the nature of your personal reality has immediate application for you. And here's why . . .

As you move ahead in your evolution—reading other self-help books, attending personal-development seminars, or consulting with your therapist—know that these activities become most valuable to you when you understand and accept that these teachers are merely mirroring the many facets of *your own being*. Knowing the truth of this is going to help you to understand and appreciate yourself much more quickly. This is a slippery concept to grasp, but grasp it you *must* if you are to finally end your outward search and achieve joy through personal autonomy.

~~~

In order for anyone's message to "sink in," there must already exist within you some corresponding energy. Otherwise there would be no basis for harmonic resonance and subsequently no communication. Let this truth help you to understand what a phenomenon you really are. What you are actually doing, in each case, when you consult any outside authority, is listening to latent, undeveloped aspects of yourself as they sympathetically vibrate to the incoming information. You then—moment-by-moment—choose which aspects of *yourself* to give the greatest voice.

You see, in your life, *you* are the authority by default, for only that to which you relate and give the greatest "ear" will prevail within your world. So-called authorities, such as therapists and authors like myself, appear to you by virtue of your good grace and consent alone, and they can disappear just as quickly. Sure, we might reflect some wonderful things back at you, and you may find yourself relating to much of the information presented. But it is up to you to hear, to accept, and to give life to the material through application.

You will be more apt to follow through with your personal growth work if you understand that as you read your books, as you communicate with your therapist, and as you attend your seminars and retreats, you are, in each case, simply talking to yourself through an intermediary.

These words which you now read are only a reminder of what, on some level, you already know. *Acting* upon that knowledge, as I am sure you have learned, is another story altogether. Action requires either great courage, or complete desperation; typically, it is prompted by a combination of the two. Perhaps you can raise your consciousness to a level where you can accept what you know. Once there, having conviction regarding that knowing is not far behind. Then, armed with that conviction, you will find the courage to act. Perhaps, in the working through of the information presented here, you can accomplish this. Perhaps not. That is your choice. Normally much trial and error needs to precede this moment of self-acceptance. That is why knowing what doesn't work (such as counting on others to rescue you) is an important prerequisite to finally trying what will work—coming to your own rescue.

All help is self-help. Without your consent and follow-through, your teachers have virtually no power to assist you. Relying on them will fail. This is where most self-help gurus or techniques turn into no help at all.

~~~

You must release the notion that someone else has the power to change your life. No matter how dynamic he or she appears or how spot-on their discourse, no other person will ever save you from yourself. Only you can do that.

Try on his or her ideas. See how well they "fit" you. Walk a mile in their shoes and see if they really get you anywhere. You will very soon, however, need to make his or her messages your own, and develop an inner coach to spur you on. This coach may take its cue from insight authors or teachers have given you, but ultimately it must be your own unique voice that inspires you.

The only way that you will finally allow yourself the power of personal authority is if you have at long last given up on the idea of being rescued by someone else.

This may be a bitter pill for many to swallow, but it is the only remedy there is for a life in paralysis. You have enough experience to know that no matter how "together" someone else is, he or she cannot live your life for you. If somewhere in the back of your mind you are still hoping to be saved, you will notice that you probably also have a tendency to want to rescue others as a sort of penance that you are willing to pay for your own rescue fantasies. You will have to drop *all* these unworkable ideas and behaviors—as true rescue is, and always has been, a solo affair. Compassion is one thing; need, quite other.

~~~

Don't be ashamed if you are still awaiting rescue. Subconsciously most of us are. In order to finally stop this damaging expectation, you will want to accept and feel some things that, until now, you may have been unwilling to admit. I repeat, if you still expect to be saved, this is a big part of your work. The sooner you get to it, the better. By the way, admission is not failure. It means: to recognize what is, and to allow it to enter—a powerfully effective "anti-ostrich" approach to life.

Admit that you did not get the love or the attention or the respect you wish you had gotten as a child. You are looking for the *experience* of this, not a denial of, or a rationalization for it. *The only reason that you still expect outside nurturing is because, on some level, you have not accepted not getting it.*

Admit whatever this makes you feel—the hurt, the anger, the sorrow, whatever it is, *feel it.*

Admit that if this has left you feeling less than good about yourself, then so be it. You know there is remedy. Admit that too.

Admit that you wish you didn't have to do now, for yourself, things that could or should have been done *for* you as a child. Accept the healthy resentment attendant to this. *Feel it.*

Admit that because of your "mishandling," your impression of yourself and your world probably needs a complete overhaul. You *will* need to do this. It will require time and patience. Don't expect overnight results. Incorporate *The Truth and the Lie Game* and The Emotional Detoxx into your life.

Admit—if much of the above is true for you—that you are habitually drawn into nonbeneficial self-talk, due to your less than stellar upbringing. Know that you will, for a time, need to monitor the inner chatter and check the validity of your negatively charged self-hypnotic messages.

Admit that no one but *you* can undo the damage that has been done. *Feel what that realization feels like.* Does that frighten you? *Admit it.*

Admit the bad news—that you are entirely in charge of your life. *Feel it.* Admit the *good* news—that you are entirely in charge of your life. *Feel that too.*

~~~

Honestly, could you say that you would be better off if you were not responsible for yourself? What control could you ever hope to exercise over getting the things you say you want? Who better to be responsible *for* you *than* you? You have first-hand, inside information about your needs and wants. You have the most to gain by virtue of your effort and the most to lose by a lack of it. No one cares as much about you as do you, nor should they. *Your life is in your hands.* Thank God. Thank yourself. Count on yourself, and count on others to do the same for *themselves.* Expecting others to have your best interests at heart (family and friends included) is naive at best, and it will lead to a lifetime of disappointment.

The shift from a helpless victim to a responsible, self-referring individual comes easier the better the original care and love one receives. But just because it is difficult does not make it impossible. This transition mainly requires an ability to diligently "stay the course," despite whatever doubts, fears, or old limiting beliefs you have that may rise up to frustrate and stop you. Know that a shift as fundamental and as profound as this does not come without courage, effort, and dedication. That way, when you get frustrated (and I can almost guarantee that you often will), you can remind yourself that this process is one of the toughest challenges most people ever face. But if you stay with it, you *will* prevail.

Your therapist—no matter how well informed or intentioned—can only lead you to the well; they cannot make you think. The multitude of articulate, intuitive therapists and self-help authors out there today may offer you a great many viable alternatives to your current way of thinking or of doing things, but they cannot implement them for you. Ultimately, they are no match for your precious beliefs.

~ ~ ~

*T*ake the *"m" out of "mother," and it's "other."*

Many of you are still waiting for the nurturing you never received as young people. You're hoping, still, to be spoon-fed your needs by some surrogate (m)other. Pardon what might be a rude awakening, but back then, back when you truly *were* at the mercy of others, was the only legitimate time to have had such an expectation. Once missed, as unfair as it is and as resentful as you may now feel about it, you are left—prepared or not—to fend for yourself. I sympathize with you, believe me, but that and twenty-five cents will get you very little nowadays.

Bemoan your fate, wallow in your self-pity, curse your inept parents, admit your anger, sorrow, resentment and guilt. Whatever it is that you are feeling, feel. Definitely welcome back *all* your feelings. Understand that this is a preparatory phase. There is little that you will actually achieve through emotional expression. But, ironically, there is little you will gain without it.

The admission and subsequent release of your feelings will have a therapeutic, cathartic effect; it will free up energy that you have been using your whole life maintaining resistance to them. This energy can then be applied in newly creative ways. Also, by admitting, welcoming, and releasing previously repressed, resisted emotion, you will be consciously creating a new void within you. And unlike the painful, unfillable, unconscious one created by your early fear or self-hate, *this* void *can* be filled, ready as you now will be to accept new self-beneficial thought and feeling energy.

~ ~ ~

One of the reasons why this work seems so difficult is that you are attempting to change the contents of your subconscious "mind." It is actually more of a full-body-thing by now; this is the reason why your habitual ways of thinking feel so much "like you." These now "body-conscious" energies were stored away at the cellular level, subsequently becoming "body belief" and yielding habitual perspectives, governing your actions and expectations. You have to learn how to outsmart your subconscious mind in order to beat it at its own game. Luckily for you, access to your subconscious belief material is through your more empirically inclined objective mind, and thus, thankfully, is malleable by virtue of an alteration of your conscious thinking.

~~~

Think of yourself as having two aspects to your consciousness. The first, the objective, is your *conscious thought activity*. It is capable of both inductive and deductive reasoning—and of having will, purpose, focus, and volition. The second, the subjective, is your *unconscious thought activity*. It is capable of deductive reasoning only. Deductive reasoning begins its activity based on an already established conclusion, simply assuming the validity of that conclusion (i.e., if A then B). It—unlike your objective thought process—cannot analyze or employ reason.

Creativity, for better or worse, lies chiefly in the hands of your subconscious, subjective processes (hence, your previous, seemingly uncontrollable "going in circles"). In order to re-direct these processes, you may not coerce or muscle them. You simply need to focus your objective will, your intention and belief, on the new "reality" you wish to create. This will impress upon your subconscious, creative aspect the "truth" of the new intent. Employing deductive reasoning only, the subconscious will assume the validity of this new conclusion—as it must and as it had the old reasoning—and then dutifully create your new condition through the Law of Attraction.

> We are surrounded by an intelligent, Creative
> Force, which acts upon our thought, but which can
> only act for us individually *through* our thought. Thus
> it automatically becomes to us what we are to It. In
> other words, It is a law of reflection. It is to us what
> we believe It to be.[17]
>
> —Ernest Holmes, *Lessons in Spiritual Mind Healing*

The problem arises when you see how limited and rigid your conscious thinking has become, due to the beliefs already held within your subconscious. You must always keep in mind, however, that no matter how ingrained or permanent your old limiting beliefs seem, they are no more a part of you than would be their more beneficial opposites. They are just more familiar.

Wisdom is the power to transcend belief. Don't be fooled by appearances. As radio personality and author Garrison Keillor says, "Sometimes you have to look reality in the eye and deny it."

Remember, too, that you are the "point of awareness," the Witness that gets to choose any new idea, any time you want to, and to consciously withdraw your attention from any old one that no longer suits you. This takes some practice and real stick-to-it-iveness. However, when you successfully alter the contents of your inner world—the world of your subjective thoughts and feelings—your life and outer conditions *must* follow suit.

~~~

Yes, freedom has a price. That price is responsibility and vigilance (thank you, Thomas Jefferson). Dependency also has a price, and that price is a loss of freedom. Which one you choose will, in large part, reflect the price you are most willing to pay. Taking responsibility, it seems to me—at least for the evolutionary minded—is the only acceptable choice. This is going to be one of the most important decisions you will ever make in your life, so by all means take your time with it. And in the process of deciding, please be gentle with yourself.

In addition, yes, *do* your complaining. Shake your fists in righteous indignation. Feel your fears, cry your tears. Then, when you have exhausted all your complaints and your reasons "why"— and you realize that you have been going round and round in circles, and are no closer to having what you want— dedicate yourself to using all that wonderful energy of yours in more self-benefiting ways.

Use the ideas and the exercises in this book. By so doing, you will come to realize Who you actually are. You will come to accept that within your universe *you* are your only hope. You will learn to guide—by your desire and will—creative energies of which you are inextricably a part. You will, at last, let everyone else off the hook, and start treating yourself with the respect, love, and kindness others were not evolved enough to offer you. And, finally, with all this progress in your personal growth, you will be well on your way to a joyful life that is filled with successful creativity!

Mystic Secret 9: Even now, you are unquestionably a huge success, in that you already have everything you most desire. By "desire," I mean that which you target most often through your intent—the overall 'focus' of your belief energy. If you don't like what you *have*, then you will need to examine, challenge, and replace your limiting beliefs.

Exercise 9: Take a look at the judgments and criticisms of yourself that you have listed in Exercises 2 and 7. See if you can notice any correlation between those opinions and beliefs and the *feelings* you routinely have or the conditions in which you typically find yourself.

For instance, if you have the belief "I don't like very many people," you will want to examine the belief "through-line" to the ensuing feeling and to the resulting condition. In this case, it's likely that you don't have very many friends. Say to yourself, "If it's true that I believe, 'I don't like very many people,' what else would I have to believe for that to be so?" Keep doing this until you have exhausted all the possibilities in that particular belief system. For instance, if the belief "I don't like very many people" yields weak "O" ring fingers—thus testing "no"—try testing "Most people don't like me."

Write your beliefs down. When you cannot come up with any additional beliefs, ask yourself, "What must I *feel* about myself in order to believe these things?" Here we are looking for the kind of feeling you probably wouldn't ordinarily want to admit to yourself. If this were not the case, it wouldn't be "hiding" from you in the first place.

Muscle-test each belief to be sure that it actually lives within you as a body-belief. These are the energies that are running you, so these are the ones you will want to access, express, and reinterpret. If what you consciously *believe* you think is not testing "yes," try testing its opposite.

Note: We often consciously assert the opposite of what we subconsciously believe when that belief is too difficult to accept head-on . . .

Example:

Belief: "I don't like very many people."
(What else would I have to believe for that to be so?)

Belief: "Most people are so stupid."
(What else would I have to believe for that to be so?)

Belief: "Well, they talk about such unimportant things."
(What else?)

Belief: "I'm just not interested most of the time."
(What else?)

Belief: "I don't have much in common with most people."
(What else?)

Belief: "I'm just different from them, so what's the point."
(What else?)

Belief: "Now that I think of it, my shyness feels a lot like embarrassment or shame."
(What else?)

Belief: "Truth is, I never did like myself much, either."
(What else?)

Belief: "O.K., O.K., I don't love myself. Are you happy now? Actually, yes. Discovering beliefs like these is incredibly important to your ultimately gaining freedom from them.

You must recognize and own them before you can release them.
Though this is only an example of what you might discover, many have reached this conclusion precisely. Once you are at the point where you can go no deeper, ask, "What must I feel about myself to believe all these things?" Feelings are the inner experiences that result from beliefs. They are felt, sensed—not thought out or conceptualized—and consequently are, by the time you discover them, almost always *irrational.*

Give yourself some time to sit with everything you have just uncovered, and let it speak to you in feelings. Try not to become too overwhelmed by what all this might *seem* to imply. It's all just the result of misinformed, misguided thought anyway.

Feeling: "I feel *unlovable.*"

Once an underriding feeling is discovered that covers and *energetically* includes everything on your belief "trail," you would then want to let yourself feel what it feels like—in this case—to be unlovable. If this is one of yours, you have probably been pushing it down or away for years. Don't be afraid of it—it's only a feeling. Run "I'm unlovable," or whatever it is that you have discovered, through The Emotional Detoxx and *The Truth and the Lie Game.* Get some objectivity on it. Even though you may be gaining a new perspective, you will still want to allow yourself the honest expression of what it *feels* like to believe you are "unlovable," or "bad," or "stupid," or "helpless," or "unworthy," or whatever your feelings may be.

Life is ironic. By not allowing the expression of these feelings you will forever be a slave to them. However, through their full expression, you can permanently leave them behind you—you can *transcend* them. This is because they are not literally true. You are not *actually* unlovable, bad, stupid, helpless, unworthy, etc. These feelings may appear very real to you, but this is only because you have not yet been fully honest with yourself.

This is precisely why *The Truth and the Lie Game* is so important. You have hidden these horrible "truths" about yourself for years, not wanting anyone to see them and thereby know what an awful thing you are. Personal integrity heals all such misperceptions. Lying to yourself about such feelings will perpetuate them. You will continue to learn more about the workings of this amazing healing machine that you are. For now, just keep doing the exercises. Shift is an experiential thing.

Weeds must be removed by the root or they will grow back. Dig as deep as you can the first time; it will save you a lot of time, energy, and heartache later on.

-40- | H.

H. is a spirited woman in her mid-twenties. She is plagued, however, with a rash of obsessive-compulsive tendencies which range from checking the gas oven ten to twenty times before leaving the house, to the endless array of worst case scenarios which she relentlessly parades before her mind's eye. H. is bright, creative, and extremely sensitive. She is efficient, caring, and methodical. Why does she suffer so?

Over the course of my personal and professional lifetime, it has become clear to me that obsessive-compulsive behavior is linked to a need to create safety. A person may think that if they can straighten their shoes at the bottom of the closet just right; line up the forks, knives, and spoons on the dinner table just so; or avoid stepping on the cracks of a sidewalk—that they will somehow be safe. In effect, they have created a sort of temporary "no fly zone," where those furious flights of anxiety can be momentarily grounded. But no sooner have they secured one fleeting fragment of well-being, then the next precarious moment is upon them, and they are once again at the frantic business of securing the next moment, and the next, and the next.

~~~

As a child, and into my young adult life, I could not be touched without developing severe anxiety. If I were touched, I would have to "touch back," in order to relieve the panic that ensued. This touching extended beyond direct contact, to floor surfaces as well. If, for instance, my foot was on a rug, and someone stepped off that rug before I could either lift my foot up or step off—they would have touched me last. This was intolerable. I would have to "get them back," by following them to whatever surface they were now on (wood, tile, carpet, etc.) and leave that area before they could. The only "safety" I seemed able to generate was one that I could artificially self-create. This continued to be the case, until I had released the repressed emotion(s) responsible for the ominous nature of my subconscious "reality." Having gone from repression to expression, an inner calm ensued, and I no longer needed to artificially fabricate external conditions as a sort of quick fix.

~~~

What is safe and what is unsafe? One person can board an airplane without a care in the world, while another imagines her certain demise. Though what is safe may be relative, the feeling of safety is a very personal, inner posture. The weak links in H.'s inner world quickly began revealing themselves to us . . . . H. was the product of a tyrant father and a doormat mother. Her father's words and actions made it apparent to the entire family that he valued his only son more highly than he did his wife or either of his daughters. The message to H. was clear: "Boys are better than girls." Additionally, Mom—being the "doormat" that she was—made a poor excuse for a female role model.

H. was stuck between a rock and a hard place. She was a girl, yet believed that *being* a girl was no great shakes. When I suggested that H. state and test, "It is my intention to be who I am," her negative response did not come as much of a surprise to me. But H. was stupefied. "You mean I don't want to be me?" she uttered in confusion. "Why would you?" I asked. "You were led to believe that this wouldn't be much to aspire to. So you didn't want to be you, and you couldn't physically, mentally, or spiritually be anyone else." Think about it. Can you imagine a more untenable position than this? Where is the foundation for such a soul? Upon what may she trust? Where may she rest?

~~~

Understandably, when I ask H. what she wants to do with her life, she is at a loss. H. has developed no inner reference point from which to give a definitive answer to such a question. An authentic experience of herself had never been available to her. She assumed that an attempt to know herself would be a worthless pursuit and consequently never learned to trust her own feelings, to let go of her incessant thought . . . To just "be."

Emotionally, in terms of self-confidence, H. was like a baby who had yet to take her first step. She was wobbly. She was scared. Her fears were literally eating her alive. When I first met H., she had just been diagnosed with "possible MS"—multiple sclerosis. I suggested to her that this might simply have been a label her doctor found convenient, as he tried to make sense out of a group of symptoms she was experiencing. These symptoms were speaking to H. (more like shouting at her), begging her to take better psycho-emotional care of herself. As expected, The Emotional Detoxx brought up a good deal of self-loathing.

Much to her credit, H. was extremely willing to explore and renegotiate these energies. Often, in crisis, people are more willing to surrender old, unworkable ideas. She has tracked down, felt, challenged, and purged. As she worked, H.'s obsessive-compulsive thoughts and behaviors, as well as her "MS"–related symptoms, gradually abated. She is now well on the way to self-recovery . . . literally in the process of recovering herself.

H. is most notably giving herself the gift of self-acceptance, and there is a corresponding inner security growing deep within her. H.'s body, now under far less stress, is returning the favor by offering back to her increased health and vitality.

For H.—as is often the case with excessively misinformed people (that would be most of us)—nearly all her thinking and behaving had to be examined and culled for its veracity and current relevance. Realizing that practically everything that one has ever believed about oneself is untrue, and that, indeed, its very opposite *is* true, can be a mind-boggling, unsettling, energy-consuming, tedious task.

But hey, have you got more important things to do?

-41- | Wanna Play Doctor?

Western-style allopathic medicine, in tandem with like-minded men and women in the pharmaceutical industry, has given us a pill for just about every symptom—psychological or physical—that occurs often enough to justify the expenses of development. Never mind that the conditions on which these firms invest millions of dollars each year are only symptomatic of deeper imbalances that ought to be receiving someone's direct attention. If they can cover them up, they're as good as gone; until, of course, through neglect, we suffer a new dysfunction, or some other related body part starts to go.

But, by then, these companies have made their fortune, and they can come up with yet more pills for the symptomatic relief of the now larger, more complicated conditions. In addition, there are all those drugs they can churn out to counter the side-effects of the ones that we've been taking. Seems like a bottomless gold mine, but me-thinks the canary keeled over a long time ago.

As an ex-asthmatic, I am all too aware of the fact that there do exist some life-saving medicines—such as corticosteroids and bronchodilators—that serve quite well *in the short term* as crisis intervention. But you would do far better to take control of this amazing "machine" of yours, learning how to keep yourself healthy—*preventatively*—or should you slip out of balance, learning how to heal yourself—naturally.

Allopathic medicine is at long last coming to terms with the fact that it is unwise to treat a condition without a careful look at the *whole* person, emotions and all, and not just the symptoms. Andrew Weil, M.D., with his roots in Western-style medicine and his branches in the more holistic Eastern traditions, is a welcome voice in the medical wilderness. In *From Chocolate To Morphine*, he and co-author Winifred Rosen state:

> " . . . Many people take drugs to relieve anxiety, depression, lethargy, or insomnia, or to escape from pain and boredom. The idea that unwanted moods are disease states treatable by taking medicines has become very popular in our society. The pharmaceutical industry has both encouraged and capitalized on this notion, with the result that the *majority* (my italics) of legal medical drugs sold today are aimed at changing undesired moods."[18]

These days, of course, we have Prozac and a whole new generation of mood elevators. For in the words of Aldous Huxley, British writer and philosopher, "Most men and women lead lives at the worst so painful, at the best so monotonous, poor, and limited, that the urge to escape, the longing to transcend themselves, if only for a few moments, is and has always been one of the principal appetites of the soul."[19] But there are many other avenues to health—The Emotional Detoxx and conscientiously applied Thought Farming for instance—with which you can help yourself physically, emotionally, and spiritually achieve a better quality of life, naturally—lessening your need and/or desire to escape.

~~~

We, as a society, really must take credit and responsibility for the tidal wave of pharmaceuticals in which we currently find ourselves drowning. We have relinquished control of our health, once again, to some "other." Tragically, not even the brightest minds of our best men and women doctors can begin to effectively maintain it for us. For health is an inside job. Unfortunately, most of us feel as though we already have one job too many.

The truth is that almost all illness, even emotional—such as depression, anxiety, and other stress-related conditions—are degenerative in nature. This means that the mind/body continuum slowly and over time succumbs to our ill-treatment. People today are, on the average, typically undernourished nutritionally, emotionally, physically, and spiritually. We simply are not offering our minds, our bodies, or our souls what they need on a regular enough basis so as to sustain ourselves in good health. This is not the AMA's fault. It is our own.

C. Norman Shealy, M.D., a Harvard-trained neurosurgeon, writes: "As a medical student I was taught that eighty-five percent of all the problems that I would ever see would be psychosomatic in nature . . . The major determinants of health—nutrition, physical exercise, and mental attitude—are not treatable by someone else but must be self-determined."[20]

Good eating habits, supplementary vitamins and minerals, moderate exercise, a meditative regime, and time spent with other evolutionarily minded people would do more for your health than could a team of Harvard Medical School doctors.

~~~

There is an inherent conflict of interest that exists in all the healing arts. Those on the "payee" side of the checks—doctors, psychotherapists, chiropractors, therapists of all sorts, and especially those who heal in a series of ongoing session work—rely on a steady stream of the dysfunctional through their offices in order to meet their basic and many of their not-so-basic needs. Face it, our dis-ease is their bread and butter.

I am not saying that there is a conscious effort on the part of those in the service of health to deliberately sabotage or prolong the healing process. But subconsciously they know that a healthy patient is an ex-patient—unless, of course, they insist that it is through *their* ongoing efforts that we maintain our good health. There may be, on their parts, subtle and some not so subtle suggestion made to us that our health is in some way dependent on co-maintenance, with they the co-partner. Even if this were so, there are some places on earth where doctors are paid for their preventative functions—such as traditional practitioners in China, for instance. There, should someone fall out of balance, these healers treat them for free. That at least seems a reasonable compromise.

I am very sensitive to this issue in my own practice, and so I deliberately go out of my way to support my client's personal authority and inner autonomy. Sometimes I feel the devil and the angel, each on one shoulder, arguing the wisdom of this behavior from a business standpoint. I comfort myself by remembering that happy clients give referrals. Also, I stay aware that it's a big world out there; it would take a very long time to help all those who either need or desire assistance.

Nevertheless, if everyone were healthy, health professionals would have to find another line of work. But we practitioners should be practicing more love and less fear. Our jobs, after all, are far from in jeopardy. Most people don't even know that their conditions, whether emotional or physical, are self-imposed. And, at least as yet, it seems that few would even wish to know this.

~~~

The road to wellness is a desolate stretch of asphalt, indeed. Oh, you'll find the occasional yoga practitioner or health food nut. But for the most part, the rest of us are all too busy running out of gas on a very different stretch of highway—destined for disaster—suffering one ailment after the next as our "machines" prematurely begin to break down.

-42- Oh God! It's Time To Talk About Spirit

In your life and therapy sessions, you have probably "gunny sacked" your woes, railing on and on about how your parents or significant others did this or didn't do that. If so, you might be absolutely correct in this interpretation of the events. The only good thing about blame though, is that, in the final analysis, you realize that it doesn't do you any good at all. You find that you are no closer to feeling better about yourself, your family, or your friends, or to achieving any of the things that you say you want. So, typically, after years of complaining, you more or less "kvetch" your way into exhaustion and, at long last, submit to a new possibility.

Any successful Thought Farmer will tell you that you can't increase the size of the harvest by blaming the weather.

Expressing resisted emotion is indeed essential to your healthy development. However, until you cease your relentless scapegoating, until you retract the pointing fickle-finger of blame, you are doomed to relive your tired old state-of-affairs. It is only when you have finally stopped blaming altogether that you may at last get a glimpse of another, infinitely more pleasant and inviting realm. As you blame less, so must you judge less. As you judge less, you begin to live a life of inclusion, rather than the one of exclusion to which you have unhappily become accustomed. **Forgiveness becomes a spiritual bridge.** The shift may initially appear to you disguised as a fleeting moment of grace, a new idea, or possibly an "impossible" dream. This is the land of "Om," the Land of Make Believe, whispering to you, telling you that greater things await, and it is cause for much hope.

~~~

You see, hope not only springs eternal, it finds its true, limitless potential at the fountain of universal Source. Essentially it is here, at the edge of this perpetual fount, that you and I are born and now stand poised as creators. To the Thought Farmer, this is his watering hole. He cannot live without it. It is this connection to Source wherein you will find purpose and the ability to satisfy that purpose.

I figure it this way: There is either a God or there is not a God. By examining the nature of the visible universe alone, it becomes clear that there is some sort of intelligence at work—undefinable perhaps—but at the very least a uniformity of design. It follows, then, that between a choice of "God or no God," it just makes sense to acknowledge the likelihood of God—some intelligent causal force. If God exists, He would need to be omnipresent—as the acorn is in every leaf of the oak. If God is "All That Is," then I am God experiencing Itself as Geoffrey Rose. If I am God-as-Geoffrey Rose, then I am energetically positioned, by birthright, to belong and to create.

I realize this is a lot of hypothetical stretching. But what if you assume the validity of all of this just long enough to examine it as a scientist might, and test out the truth of these fabulous notions for yourself? That would make sense wouldn't it? No one is asking that you swallow all this unchallenged—hook, line, and sinker. I do ask, though, that you keep an open mind, and allow the truth to make itself known to you. For the sake of this experiment, you simply need to accept the *possibility* of God. O.K?

O.K. Here's the pitch . . . .

Just beyond the reach of your five senses—within and around you—exists a sheltering, omnipresent "oasis." Here, according to both ancient and current metaphysical thinking, in what proves a causal dimension, you and I connect to that which creates, animates, and sustains us, protected by the immutable Law of Belonging.

This is the "Oneness" in which everyone and everything has its rightful place. The world's great Thought Farmers are frequent visitors here. It is an alternate, simultaneous reality, where nonconditional life is lived. Here you remain, as ever, untouched, unbeaten, never having been asked to be anything but authentically "you." This causal domain is home to the underlying nature of all life. By touching it, you will, in essence, establish a through-line to your basic, causal Self. It is here, after all, that your physical self has its genesis, in metaphysical origin.

After you have experienced this "place," you will never again be tempted to measure your worth in dollars or accomplishments. These may indeed remain desirable, but you will understand that they cannot compensate you for the poverty of "separateness." Those that "have" know on some level the limited value of their possessions. One may accumulate many "things" in life, but these do not create joy, fulfillment, or a greater sense of self-worth. These wonderful conditions are established only if you develop a relationship with Source and begin to realize that you are "It." Yes, that "It" is you, and that *here* is your worth, your power, and your purpose.

~~~

What you are in the process of doing is "returning" to a place you have never actually left. But since this is a place you have never *consciously* been before, it shouldn't come as much of a surprise to you if you find yourself doubting its existence. Yes, it is true that you *are* this place, undifferentiated, and that a return to "all-of-you" is where you are headed. But yours is an evolving consciousness. The "all-of-you" that you began to systematically abandon as a child is not the "all-of-you" you are returning to as you reintegrate. Don't get too caught up in the explanation of all this. You are heading for new experiences, and experiences must be experienced. Just give these new ideas some time.

Recapturing Zoe's fun-loving, child's-eye intuitive belief in goodness—a quality you have lost and now seek to regain—is certainly an important aspect of this homecoming. But you want to be child*like*, not child*ish*. Early in life, we don't differentiate between thou and I. But this is not the state of "nonduality," or Oneness, that one reaches for in transcendence. No infant has the capacity for Universal Consciousness. There is actually little that these near polar-opposite evolutionary stages have in common. One is pre-conscious, the other super-conscious. One, Narcissistic (undifferentiated me/you); the other, cosmic-conscious (nonduality). One, egocentric; the other, ego-transcendent or world-centric.

By creating a rapport with Source and establishing a mature, ego-transcendent, world-centric view, you will begin to experience the confidence-through-belonging that you are going to need in order to successfully Thought Farm. Here, through new-found awareness, you will start to feel "whole," intact, integrated, and connected, with no further need or desire to blame or accuse. (For instance, with this elevated awareness, God-as-Geoffrey Rose would have no one to blame but himself, would he?)

Achieving this perspective, as you will see, will genuinely feel like an evolutionary milestone. Though elusive as it may now seem to you, this "state" is actually more real than any feeling or belief you have ever had. And, though real as it is, this is a "castle-in-the-clouds-like" kind of place, where the shifting winds of your attitudes and perspectives continually blow it in and out of view. The connection is always there, but seldom seen.

This personal paradise, if you will, periodically calls to you, riding in on a breeze that has, somehow, opportunistically slipped through a momentary "open window" in your otherwise walled-up fortress of fear, anger, guilt, or sorrow. It's the "vacationer's mentality," where both worry about the past and anxiety about the future take a holiday, and you are left face to face with a Here and Now experience.

You see, sometimes you forget how angry, sad, or scared you are. You may be distracted for a moment, and the world has a chance to touch you directly, not having to penetrate your skepticism, analysis, and standard-issue emotional armor. This unfiltered, nonjudged, unintellectualized bit of experience can "happen" to you in the haze of a sunset or the twinkle of a new-born's eyes. It catches you off guard, and you momentarily find yourself "at-one-with." This moment of "strength through belonging" is the solid footing, the sense of well-being and grace that you long to recapture and maintain. It is the very ground that you, as a successful Thought Farmer, will want to homestead and cultivate.

How can you mine these moments of Oneness, string them together side by side into a necklace of perpetual Now? How can you learn to trust ongoingly in life and your ability to successfully meet whatever challenges it offers you next? How do you discover and stay in "flow"—that "place" that is home to the writer's muse, the lover's gaze, and the athlete's "zone"?

The answer to these questions cannot be found through any mental process. It cannot be deduced. Any quest for self-hood, purpose, or "flow" that is led principally by your analytical mind—intellect filtering experience to the point of *non*-experience—will leave you with a sense of disconnection, isolation, and separateness. Again, not much inspiration for getting out of your warm bed in the morning.

The only way that you will ever accomplish this for yourself is if you find practical application for the ideas brought forth here. You have lived a lifetime believing one set of "truths." You know what results you have achieved. It's time to try on some new ideas. Accept my "God-as-you" argument for a while. Try it on for size. Prove or disprove *for yourself* which beliefs lead you to the pit of despair, and which to the pot of gold at the end of the rainbow.

-43- | One Lousy Apple

Backtracking down the evolutionary trail . . . In the story of Adam and Eve, our momentarily happy couple defies God's edict and eats the fruit of the Tree of the Knowledge of Good and Evil. We are told that this act of defiance triggers the fall from grace and humankind's subsequent need to leave the garden forever. Seems a rather harsh punishment for one moment of indiscretion. Yet, as our tenacious, judgmental natures would suggest, the banishment remains in full force. What was so "forbidden" about this mythological fruit, and why did eating it prove to be so disastrous?

Good and evil. Right and wrong. Our "knowledge" of any distinction proves to be the precursor for all judgmental thinking. Bias, prejudicial thought, feelings of non-deservedness, perfectly illustrate and exemplify our fall from grace and Eden, that primordial garden of favor and freely given, unmerited love of God, ourselves, and each other.

~~~

After the fall, consider the fall-out: Inherent in every thought, every spoken word, and every action (which we shall call "cause") is some probable "effect," some "result." This is what Christ means, when he says, "As ye sow, so shall ye reap." This eternal law creates a sort of automatic punishment/reward system which dictates, among other things, that if you give too much emphasis to segregating your life into good and evil aspects, you lose your inherent natural integrity, wherein there never was nor could be this distinction. Hence, divisiveness—the loss of integrity (wholeness)—becomes its own "punishment" by virtue of how dislocated it makes you feel. Duality, nested in this "knowledge of good and evil," is the stuff of our deepest emotional strife—me/you, right/wrong, good/bad—this is the breeding ground for nearly all our fear and anger.

Even if we assume that Adam and Eve's story is pure parable, the condition in which we humans still find ourselves doesn't seem fundamentally fair. The punishment just doesn't seem to fit the crime; not unless we are some way in control of a reprieve ourselves. I have learned that the timing of this merciful reprieve does, indeed, lie fully with us. This is a key fact every aspiring Thought Farmer must come to realize.

~~~

It is written that "God made man in His own image." This must surely be one of the most telling, challenging, and controversial statements handed down through scripture. What could it possibly mean? That we resemble God physically? Or that in some greater way we are God-like?

> "In Persia, the name of the fabulous huma bird is derived from the root, *Hum*, which is related to OM. . . . *Hu* is a direct reference to the Word of God. In 'human,' the *man* portion comes from the Sanskrit Mana, or 'mind of the ordinary man.' So the term 'human' is therefore an eternal reminder . . . that God is even now in all men, and can be more fully realized by all."[21]
>
> —David Tame, *The Secret Power Of Music*

To the ever-inquisitive little boy still living within me, whose "telescope" remains symbolically fixed to the heavens, it has become crystal clear that it is my capacity to create-at-will that lies central to the remarkable resemblance I seem to have to that which created me. Creativity and free will appear to be the divine tools with which I can either build my own heaven—and return to Eden—or create my own hell, by personally continuing the banishment.

Telescope, microscope, or no scope at all, as I scan about, I am aware of myself scanning about. I am aware of my thoughts and the energetic realms to which they usher me. I am conscious of my consciousness. In my awareness, I mistakingly distinguish myself from that which I am aware, no longer satisfied to merely "belong." Then, as surely as night must follow day, I fall . . . I fall from the grace of Oneness into the pit of "Good and Evil," the prison of "Me vs. You," the dungeon of chaotic despair, and the swamp of FEAR. Could this be where it all starts to unravel, where all my fears and doubts have their root? Probably, yes. But in any case, I must ultimately choose whether I want to live with the ensuing pain, numb myself through some obsessive act or addictive substance, or try to make order out of my self-perpetuated personal bedlam.

In this exercise of personal choice, there seems a rather striking resemblance to what we are told was God's first creative act . . . "When darkness was on the face of the deep . . ." when the universe was in *its* state of primordial disarray. *The Old Testament* begins, "In the beginning, God created the heavens and the earth. The earth was without form, and void; and darkness was on the face of the deep. And the Spirit of God was hovering over the face of the waters. Then God said, 'Let there be light,' and there was light." This, we are told, was the very first act of creation—creation at its genesis. I, too, seem to possess this fantastic ability to *create*. For instance, I say, "I will write a book," and there is a book—creation at its momentary periphery.

In no way do I believe this comparison to be blasphemous. After all, it is the creator "above" that makes possible the creator "below." If God made man in His own image, then He made me in His image as well. And if this is so, there must be evidence for it. Exhibit A, the book you hold in your hands. But writing this book does not necessarily bring me any closer to divine love, peace, or wisdom. The book, then, is merely the result of having found a way to exercise some Divine muscle, to allow some God-like quality of play into my life.

An illumined consciousness, creativity, and choice, it now seems, mutually hold the keys to the Grail castle and divine kinship, and they are basic to the character, and essential to the development, of every great Thought Farmer.

-44- | Eden Was Only a Garden– You Are the Gardener

"Creative ability," as herein defined, is different from the miracle of procreation, which seems more an endless echo of God's sixth-day pronouncement, "Let Us make man in Our image." Creation perpetually regenerates, renewing Itself in spirited recreation. Sex is Fun. Call me master of the obvious, but this is truly genius at work. However, the types of creative acts to which I now refer are the willful, purposeful directives we give ourselves that lead to manifestation by intent. These are the very roots of Thought Farming. Could it be that the Bible, rather than being an historical document, is a coded manual, a "how-to," a tutorial on creativity?

Beavers build dams and birds build nests, but these acts are instinctual; the animals are driven, they are not the drivers. The Canadian Goose, for instance, cannot decide one day to plug up a river, nor can the beaver choose to head south for the winter. These animals simply don't have the wherewithal. Their decisions are genetically dictated, etched, hard-wired deep within them.

My creative acts, on the other hand, though they may be directed somewhat by genetic tendency, are not limited by biological imperatives. They stem from personal, unique desire and choice. Today I may feel the urge to write a poem. If my intent is strong enough, I will have a poem by day's end. My creations seem to grow from the soil that is my personal creative force, watered by my intention. This perpetually fertile ground will yield practically an infinite crop variety of action/result; my harvest today, a direct consequence of what I planted yesterday.

It is likely that Adam received his name from the Hebrew word Adamah, meaning "soil" or "ground." In this one word, "Adam," the first name given mankind, we may witness our heritage—to be of the earth. And we may witness our destiny—to be fruitful. The decision to grow one thing instead of another becomes our "crop" choice, made of our own free will. If only we all had the clean-slate choice field of a Tiger Woods, who "knows no boundaries inside himself." Imagine, a world of super-achievers. Actually, there would be no such creatures at all, for the full use of potential would be commonplace.

I suppose it could be argued that I, like the beaver and the goose, am programmed, coerced by genetic predisposition, societal pressure, parental conspiracy, or by any number of other internal or external imprints. But even if this were so, my ability to change my mind and choose anew squarely places me in the role of initiator. Like it or not, my life is my creation.

But I digress. If it is true that I am created in the image and likeness of God, and that this resemblance means that I, too, am a creator, why then can't I simply "poof" myself into a state of perpetual grace? Well, perhaps I can. But before I try, it might be a good idea to have a better understanding of the workings of creativity itself.

~~~

If I am, as it is beginning to appear, the gardener, what can I plant so as to grow my personal Eden back? In *A New Design for Living*, Ernest Holmes and Willis H. Kinnear state:

> " . . . energy and mass are interchangeable . . . the
> practical physicist has demonstrated this. Nobel Prize
> winning physicist Werner Heisenberg stated ' . . . there
> is only one fundamental substance of which all reality

consists . . . 'energy.'"[22] They continue, "Mind . . . appears to be the ultimate source of energy, and energy is Mind in action. Energy is the essence of atoms. Atoms are the building blocks of every physical thing. Thoughts are things. And all is in perfect accord with law . . . ."[23]

This seems as likely a description of the way things are as any I have yet encountered. I especially like the wording because it leaps from the theoretical into the practical, by suggesting mind as tool. It implies that there are ways of using that tool in the service of creation. Accordingly, the crop you harvest—your "reality"—will be a product of your mental energy . . . this most basic of things. And how do you gain mastery over something so esoteric as the laws governing creative manifestation? You must first examine the effect that these principles are having on your life.

As an example: In the case of my asthma, my intense desire to be rid of it already included a powerful secret component— the belief that I could be me *and* asthma-free simultaneously. Taking this a step further, this also included the idea that I was, on some level, *already* non-asthmatic (back to the elephant in the stone—the asthma being a part of the stone). Accepting the concept that good health was at least as real a possibility as my poor health had been proved essential to the healing process. Voicing my intent, "I'd like to get rid of my asthma," proved vital as well, as this amplified my intention. Creating this new ideological vantagepoint set up a fresh energetic vibration within me. This, in turn, was met with a corresponding frequency in the physical world, manifesting both as my radiant friend, with her story of new-found health, and Stephanie Ewings, the healer I needed to meet.

-45- | Imagine That!

Remember our friends: enthusiasm, joy, spontaneity, and unconditional love? These are essential "elephant" attributes, yet many of us have only a vague recollection of them. Some have no memory of them at all. But whether we consciously remember them or not, we are surely homesick for them. For these are the emotional equivalents of the smell of cinnamon rolls and coffee, or bacon and eggs that no longer waft into our sleepy bedrooms through the early morning air, and we miss them terribly.

Well, if you are ready, like Bob Dylan says, "It's a new morning," and this time the kitchen is all yours. The old adage, "If you want something done right, you'd better do it yourself," applies doubly to personal growth and happiness. But how do we begin to cook up or recapture a way of being or feeling that we can hardly remember or, by means of socialization or our adult "logic," we have relegated to the realm of the naive, fantastic, and impossible? Most of us would expect that nothing short of a miracle could pry us loose from our current conditions and skepticism. How do we begin to create something totally new out of our tired old raw material?

~~~

The answer to this is evolution . . . *personal* evolution. Evolution is the process of bringing into form "more"; it's mining the infinite, essentially via Thought Farming. It's been going on for millennia, hidden in plain view, cloaked in metaphysical, mystical attire. You need simply to sharpen, then learn to use your God-given tools. You need to develop the eyes to see, the ears to hear, the intelligence to interpret, and the intuition to sense that which is, and has always been, going on within and around you—albeit on an invisible, causal level.

"Invisible level? Oh, great. How are we supposed to deal with that?" you might be thinking. Well, don't let this little detail throw you. Just because you cannot see the Law of Gravity does not mean that it is not there. Right? The *effect* of gravity is the proof of its existence. So, too, it is with the Laws of Mind and Spirit which govern creative manifestation. The mechanics of these laws lie beyond the scope of your five senses, too. You must, therefore, look to *their* effect when getting the heft of, and learning to wield, the invisible tools with which you have been divinely gifted for "reality" building.

Like gravity, just because belief and emotion are invisible, it does not mean that they are inconsequential. An honest look at your life will certainly convince you of this, for it is a perennially faithful expression of what you think and feel.

~~~

Just as soon as you have begun your release work, "clearing the land" of your old emotional resistance, you can begin to consider some new options. Know, however, that until you have energetically made room within yourself for these new ideas, they will not take root, and you will typically meet with little more than frustration and disappointment. The reason? Just as in the physical world, within the inner realm of thoughts and feelings, no two "objects" can occupy the same space at the same time. You cannot believe, for instance, that you are about to meet the "man of your dreams," while simultaneously believing that you are unworthy of happiness.

Just the other day, I was with a client who uncovered an old limiting belief that stood squarely in her way. I had asked this entrepreneurial sort what it was she wanted (by the way, this is always a good question to ask *yourself*). Her response to me was, "I want to be making a million dollars a year." I said, "O.K., let's see if your 'body beliefs' support you on this." In no time at all we had uncovered an imbalance related to this notion, indicating that she was resisting an old fear of some kind. Through muscle testing, we discovered that this fear was related to her father in some way. "Well," she said, "he *did* always say that I had to be the best at everything, and that because I was a woman, and a black woman on top of that, I would have to work much harder than most people to get what I wanted."

"Hmmm," I offered in my best doctoral style, "Do you think that that message frightened you?" "I suppose it did," she said, "but I'm sure my Dad only wanted to protect me by telling me 'How it was out there.'" "Perhaps," I concurred, "but he planted a very scary thought in you, didn't he? Do you think that this could explain your aborted attempts to get ahead and your tendency to procrastinate?" "Definitely," she chimed, the light bulb finally going on. "Having to be the best all the time is a huge responsibility. That, coupled with the idea that because I'm a black woman I'm somehow handicapped . . . now I can see how crippling my father's message actually was."

All that was left for this brave soul to do was to face her fears related to her gender and race, and their attendant hardships. These fears had remained hidden away since early childhood behind what she had always assumed was her father's good advice. With these fearsome beliefs felt, challenged, and out of the way, she is now no longer paralyzed—either by having to be the best all the time or by assuming that both her race and her gender are inherent liabilities. When retested, her body no longer "disagreed" with her desire to be making a million dollars a year. She had made room for that possibility within her and, within a month, had found a better, higher-paying job.

Once the idea "weeds" have been cleared from the mind field, Thought Farmers have a magical tool to help them plant and grow new life conditions. Actually, it only seems magical because its mechanics are currently beyond the scope of our understanding. This, however, in no way diminishes its power, nor makes its phenomenal results any less real. This mystical tool is one that we will use again and again. It is our imagination.

The Mirriam Webster Dictionary defines "imagination" as: "1: the act or power of forming a mental image of something not present to the senses, or not previously known or experienced. 2: creative ability."[24]

Through the imagination, Thought Farmers can actually begin planting *before* physically managing a homecoming. Quietly at work in my decision to let go of my asthma, for example, was an energy signifying that I had at least begun to *imagine* myself without it. This is what Stephanie Ewings understood and was referring to when she said, "Because you're ready to give it up."

~~~

In order to successfully use your imagination, you must first be willing to admit that your limiting beliefs may be misguided and that, indeed, their very opposite may be true. This proves a bigger step to take than most would expect, and that is why *The Truth and the Lie Game*, the "letting go" exercise, and The Emotional Detoxx are so important. We tend to use our beliefs, for better or worse, as floatation devises. We clutch onto them for dear life, tragically assuming that we would be sunk without them, that somehow our very lives depend upon maintaining them.

It is much more accurate to say, however, that we are sunk if we *don't* challenge them and let them go. Remember the discussion of fingernail clippings and the various other things that you are not? Well, you are *not* your beliefs, not any of them. Keep questioning yours, and you won't have to take my word for it.

~~~

Once you successfully suspend a limiting belief (see exercise at the end of this chapter), imagining or visioning becomes your next most important Thought Farming "implement." When you are able to imagine something vividly enough, meaning to the point that you temporarily but honestly *feel* as though it is true for you, then—within the context of your inner-world—it becomes "real." Spend enough time in this new mindset, and you will begin to change the "balance-of-power." This is due to the fact that imagination works in accordance with the Law of Correspondence, "As within, so without." Hence, once your inner posture reaches a point of critical mass, taking you to a new energetic place, the corresponding outer conditions must begin to manifest. This is because you are an intrinsic, hologramistic, part of "All-That-There-Is," and can therefore directly affect It.

The exact nature of that manifestation is not always certain. Sometimes I am amazed at how close my creation comes to my original vision, but more often than not, I am a bit surprised by the result. For example: Several years ago, I had decided to expand my horizons *vis-à-vis* women. I thought it would be a good idea if I dated someone from another culture, so I meditated and visualized the type of woman I was interested in meeting.

I built her in my mind—much like my own Frankenstein monster, albeit prettier and female. I was as specific as I could be: She was European, five-foot-two to five-foot-five—dark haired, slim, and extremely good-natured. She had a sweet, pretty face, smelled great and, most importantly, she would *feel* good, both in my life and in my arms.

I knew that I wanted to exercise my nurturing muscles in my

next relationship, as I had typically been in relationships wherein the woman was the nurturer. So, in my mind, I created someone I could help mold—someone both young and new to the American way of life. In addition to the visualization work that I knew I must do, I asked my friends to be on the lookout for such a woman.

A few weeks after I had put the imagination process into high gear, a friend told me that he had met someone who he thought I might find interesting. We arranged to meet at a local restaurant—a French place with an extremely popular bar scene. The night I was to meet my "monster," I joined my friend and his date at the bar. An hour or so passed . . . and no show. Then, there she was. A pretty brunette . . . *but she had come with a date.* No one had told her that this night had been arranged for us to meet—they had merely invited her down to join us for drinks, not wanting to scare her off with a match-making overture.

The evening was a bust. I couldn't get close enough to talk to or to get to know this woman in any fashion whatsoever. There was, however, something about her that I could sense from a distance that reminded me of the picture I had painted in my mind. Nothing too precise—just a reminiscent energy. But the night would pass, my curiosity unreconciled.

Weeks later, the same friend threw himself a birthday party, and he decided to give the introduction yet another try. This time, my friend let the mystery woman know that he was inviting someone whom he wanted her to meet. And this time, she came alone—doubtful, but curious. We were introduced and began to talk, and I searched her face and personality for evidence of a sign that this girl was *the* girl I had built in my mind. Close, I thought—really close. She was slender, around five-foot-five, mid-twenties, bright, pretty, raven-haired, and very good-natured. She told me that she had only been in the United States for a couple of years, and that she had come to Los Angeles with her entire family—consisting of her grandmother, mother, father, and sister.

I listened to her accent . . . definitely foreign, but I couldn't put my finger on it. I soon learned that Valerie was a Russian immigrant, here to escape religious persecution. She had as yet made no real inroads into the American way of life, still "hanging-out" exclusively with other Russian immigrants. Her English was quite good, however, considering her short length of time here. Valerie explained that her grandmother had taught English in Russia, and that she had gotten a head start on it years before.

We took our conversation outside for a little quiet. The air was clear and a bit cool by California standards, and Valerie shuddered when she hit the night chill. I gently put my arms around her to keep her warm. In that moment, I received my sign. As I ever so gently held Valerie close to me, a lovely, healing energy washed through me—an energy I had never quite experienced before. This was the sign I had been waiting for.

~ ~ ~

Over the course of the next several years, Valerie and I built a lovely relationship. We lived together for several of those years, and during that time, I helped Valerie grow into a more confident, fully enculturated American citizen. The relationship proved perfect for us both. I was able to learn from her—to learn how to care for her, to give to her, to exercise my patience, and to experience how it felt to be around someone from a different culture. I worked my giving muscles in all the ways that I had hoped to and in some I could never have imagined. She, on the other hand, got to really dig into American soil. She met friends through me, got a job through those connections, and slowly but surely learned the ways of the West.

Each of us was just what the other needed at the time. Then, after having satisfied all the reasons for which we had gotten together, Valerie moved out on her own. The decision was mutual and just as natural as the one that had brought us together in the first place. Today, we remain good friends, forever a part of each other's lives and evolution.

~~~

Valerie matched up pretty closely with my imaginary girl. But you must remember that in your early imagination work the reflection might not be quite so clear. For you are "painting" with energy. Sometimes you are using a very fine brush and can come up with some amazing detail work. But more likely than not, you are using a considerably larger brush, producing broad, sweeping, unrefined energetic strokes. The resultant life "portrait" may be less the perfect likeness of your hopes and dreams, and more typically the abstraction of them.

Another metaphor that might help you appreciate the elusive nature of the creative process is if, when you use your imagination, you presume that you are "knocking" on manifestation's door. If you knock loudly and often enough, something or someone *will* show up at the door. Exactly who or what is not entirely certain. Or they or it may actually appear at another door behind you, one that you had not even noticed, and that you had, not consciously at least, been knocking on at all. Something, however, will happen. Energy *must* beget energy. Your efforts are never, can never, be in vain. You may not always get exactly what you are "knocking" for, but you will get something which physically matches the "complexion" of your predominant energetic intent.

Again, I invite you to examine the nature of your life and then to compare it to your beliefs. Your life is a reflection, a sometimes darkly diffused, sometimes crystal clear mirror image, of your most deeply held thoughts and feelings—your perspectives and imaginings. Make sure that you have an appreciation of this. It will inspire you to continue to review and revamp those limiting beliefs of yours.

~~~

One last word on the subject of imagination . . . doubt works on the same principle. This is why learning to suspend your disbelief plays such a vital role in creating any new conditions for yourself. If you cannot imagine (meaning: "sincerely doubt") that you can do something, you will either convince yourself not to try it, or somehow foil the attempt. The result will be the same as if you really were unable to do it. You may know this phenomenon by the name "self-fulfilling prophesy." Whatever you call it, it is merely the "coming into form"—the manifestation of belief. The good news is that the very same energies that can inhibit you from getting the things you want, a reality with which you may be all too familiar, can be harnessed for the sake of personal achievement.

Mystic Secret 10: *Imagination is the well from which all creation drinks; life—an ever-changing tapestry—a work-in-progress on the frontiers of fantasy.*

Exercise 10: Here, you will want to expand upon what you currently think of as "possible" for yourself, without losing believability altogether. This, therefore, becomes an exercise of incremental gain. It is, for example, far easier for a child to imagine himself walking *after* completing his first step, than before he had first pulled himself to his feet. These "steps" become important vista points on the way to anywhere new, for you typically will not generate anything that you are unable to imagine.

Begin meditating. After you have reached a deep level of relaxation in your meditation—or if you do not yet meditate, relax using whatever method that works best for you—"introduce yourself" to something you would soon like to achieve or acquire. This will entail your creating a mental image of what you want, incorporating as many details into that picture as you can. You will want to make this as life-like as possible. Your "goal" might relate to career, your living situation, a relationship with someone you love, a health issue, or a monetary objective—pick some relatively small desire that you would like to see fulfilled fairly quickly.

Initially, it is wise to choose a goal that doesn't require too much of a belief stretch. In this way, when you create that detailed picture in your mind and imagine what it feels like to have it *right now* (be it that new job, boyfriend, house, good health, or whatever), you will be able to minimize the doubt that is sure to rise up and greet you from the front line of your fantasy.

Focus on it clearly, but gently. It should feel like a lovely, dreamy gift that you are offering yourself. Recognize, but "rope in," any doubts that come along. You can do so by gently reminding yourself that this is an experiment in creating something brand new and that your doubts have had more than their share of your time and energy—yielding less than satisfactory results.

Affirmations can be useful. They can help you to reprogram your subconscious mind, and to set new chains of causation into motion. Borrowing once again from Shakti Gawain, here are some examples of affirmations you might choose to incorporate into your belief work:

Set One:
It's O.K. for me to have everything that I want.
I am whole and complete in myself.

Set Two:
I am dynamically self-expressive.
I am now attracting loving, satisfying, happy relationships into my (personal and professional) life.

Set Three:
The more I have, the more I have to give.
The more I give, the more I receive, and the happier (and healthier) I feel.

In her book *Creative Visualization*, Gawain explains: "Always phrase affirmations in the present tense, not in the future. It's important to create it as if it *already exists*. Don't say: 'I *will* get a wonderful new job,' but rather: 'I now have a wonderful new job.' This is not lying to yourself; it is acknowledging the fact that everything is created *first* on the mental plane, before it can manifest in objective reality."[25]

An important fact to remember about affirmations is that there exists a hierarchy to them. In other words, if you cannot affirm, meaning "make firm," the belief, "It's O.K. for me to have the things that I want," you are going to have a hard time creating much else. Success with Set One–type affirmations will make possible success with Set Two–type affirmations, which in turn will make possible success with Set Three–type affirmations.

Use *The Truth and the Lie Game* to help yourself gain objectivity and more of a neutral stance toward those feelings and beliefs that are affirmation-resistant. Remember, all you have to do is *suspend* your disbelief, you do not have to fully dismiss it, nor must you permanently convince yourself of its opposite. Success with the earlier "letting go" exercise in Chapter 29 would pay off in spades here, as you would not have to go through each belief one at a time. Having an *experiential* appreciation of the fact that you are neither your beliefs, nor they you, would turn these exercises into creative forays.

Affirmations must always be in the affirmative. Say, "I am in perfect health," not "I'm *not* sick anymore." Manifestation responds to creative intent in the form of energy and words symbolizing that energy. "I am in perfect health" energetically says "health." "I am not sick anymore" energetically says "sick." **You attract both what you assert and what you resist— so be careful.**

Affirmations are also a good way of finding your hidden sabotaging beliefs, so don't beat yourself up if you are unable to imagine or affirm the things you say you want. Turn this inability into a friend who is helping you to locate your hidden limiting beliefs. Work first on the ones that seem the most foundational. Use your Thought Farming tools. Be resourceful. It's going to pay off in more ways than you are currently able to . . . *imagine.*

| # "If You Build It, 'He' Will Come"

As I illustrated earlier, when I was a young boy I was riddled with self-doubt. For the most part, this meant that I experienced very little joy and a virtual freeze on getting the things I thought I wanted. However, every now and then, I would long for something with more passion than usual. On those rare occasions, I always, and to my utter amazement, got what I hungered for. It seems that when my desire "outweighed" my doubt, my imagination was allowed to fly. I can recall thinking at the time how incredible my "batting average" became when I allowed myself to get passionate about something.

There seemed to be some aspect of my passion that enabled me to see through the maze of "what ifs" and "why bothers" and to devise a plan that had a high probability of success. When I focused on the goal, the path to that goal became clear. When I focused on the impediments to that goal, the path seemed more and more dangerous, less and less inviting. Passion seemed to keep my climber's focus on the "heights" of having and off the "looking down" into the potential for disaster.

**Passion is our rocket fuel as we
shoot for the stars.**

Metaphysicians claim that there is a Universal Mind into which our thoughts go and from which manifestation finds its form. I believe that this is true, and I feel that this is, indeed, how I "created" my careers, my health, and so many of my other life's successes. However I am equally convinced that selective perception is always operative, and that when I allow myself the opportunity of visionary thinking—rehypnotizing myself so to speak—I give myself license to discover new, workable solutions. Let's look at how passion might fit into all of this.

The following may sound trivial to you, but to a man who started life off feeling completely skeptical and totally ineffectual, it recounts a decisive moment . . . Back in the early 1960s, when I was just ten or so, Jerry Lewis's Muscular Dystrophy campaign efforts won an early place in my young heart. I became impassioned about helping in some way. It was possible to put on Muscular Dystrophy Carnivals to raise money to help fight the disease, so I decided that I would organize such an event.

I had absolutely no idea how I was going to accomplish this feat. Nevertheless, thoughts began coming to me; ideas for various carnival games began to appear in my mind as I let myself fantasize and see the event "up and running" in my imagination. Using odds and ends I found in the storage closet and garage, I designed games of chance from the images appearing in my mind. Tossing ping-pong balls into empty milk bottles and hitting a croquet ball through a single hoop strategically placed for difficulty were two events I can recall "inventing."

Once planned, I would need to attract customers. I hung hand-written flyers all over the neighborhood announcing the time, date, and place of my carnival for charity. I was not an overly popular kid, nor extroverted for that matter, so I couldn't rely on any preexistent goodwill. I was flying solo, never having had even a single flying lesson.

To make a long story short, the carnival was a huge success. I charged one penny per try and raised over twenty dollars for Jerry's kids. I was amazed at my achievement. It was a huge win for me, proving that if I set my mind to something, I could achieve it. With my eye "glued" to the goal, I had never allowed myself to consider failure. **Success was imminent, because it had already completely occurred in my mind.**

This sort of "fluke" win became a pattern in my life—only, however, when I was sufficiently impassioned. In college, I ran for school office against a field of far more "in" young people. But because I *truly* wanted to win, I was able to see the platform upon which I needed to stand in order to assure a victory. I won by a substantial margin.

Ernest Holmes, a pioneer in metaphysics and the author of *The Science of Mind*, writes, "When we (create) we do not wish, we KNOW. We do not dream, we STATE. We do not hope, we ACCEPT. We do not pray, we ANNOUNCE. We do not expect something is going to happen, we BELIEVE THAT IT HAS ALREADY HAPPENED."[26]

I had somehow gotten all of this right—by accident.

It was only sometime after graduation from college that I began to understand what I had been doing all along. I hadn't yet enjoyed that many wins, but I could see that the ones that I did have had elements in common: *Passion was key.* Allowing for the possibility of what I wanted was critical (suspending disbelief). Intent and focus were indispensable. Lastly, taking action on the ideas that began to bubble up from within me also played an essential role.

Knowing these things enabled me to achieve with great confidence—whenever passion filled me. Unfortunately, most of the time I felt rather *blasé* about life. Because of this, my successes were few and far between. Over the years, I became convinced that I could not rely on my intermittent passion if I were to have a life where achievement was more the norm than the exception.

I would need to devise a method for creating under the conditions imposed by my "usual" state of mind—or change my state of mind. As an inexperienced Thought Farmer, I had had random luck. My successes, though real enough, were sporadic. My approach to creativity back then was akin to intermittently and haphazardly raising only the one crop that I happened to love growing, cooking, and eating, while leaving the rest of my nutritional needs unmet. As good as they are, man cannot live by sweet potatoes alone.

~~~

Taking into account the conditions under which my early successes were achieved, I began designing an approach to creativity that would cover all the same bases, passion or no. But almost immediately, it occurred to me that passion was one thing I really did not want to be without. My initial efforts, therefore, became an attempt to create a sort of passion "umbrella" for my life.

I accomplished this feat slowly, over a period of years of trial and error, by ultimately employing techniques that allowed for more and more contact with the Here and Now. One of the first steps I took was to buy myself a motorcycle. I'll tell you this—if you're not "in the moment" on a bike, you're history. I also started acting classes. Sandy Meisner's scriptless "moment-to-moment" exercises helped me to experience what Now *feels* like. These I recommend. The motorcycle, on the other hand, is a highly personal choice.

Mindfulness practice also proved key to unlocking the passion door. In meditation, I found that when I was Here and Now, life felt great—just like I always knew it could. This process involved developing an enhanced level of awareness. Awareness, unlike analysis, is intellectually passive. There is no "work" involved in it, *per se*. This is more the stuff of neutral observation, requiring no effort other than that of "letting go"; somehow, though, it is experientially very active. Initially I was able to sustain this energetic stance only during my meditation or fantasy time.

However, the more that I practiced it, the more able I was to bring this "lively peace" into my daily life. What happens as you do any mindfulness exercise is that you become more and more present. The more present you allow yourself to be, the more you get to experience a delightful sort of euphoria, where almost everything quietly takes on an amusing entertainment value. This is because, as we have seen, thinking and feeling don't mix. So when you are in an experiential mode, there is little chance for your old judgmental thinking to come in and crash the party. Experience without judgment feels great ninety-nine percent of the time. It is almost always our thinking (worrying, doubting, and angsting) that spoils what would otherwise be a naturally pleasant, mildly euphoric sensation— that being a direct experience of the Here and Now. This is why focused activity of *all* kinds is so enjoyable.

In discussing the results of his research on the elements of enjoyment, Mihaly Csikszentmihalyi reports:

> "The first surprise we encountered in our study was how similarly very different activities were described when they were going especially well. Apparently the way a long-distance swimmer felt when crossing the English Channel was almost identical to the way a chess player felt during a tournament or a climber progressing up a difficult rock face. All these feelings were shared, in important respects, by subjects ranging from musicians composing a new quartet to teenagers from the ghetto involved in a championship basketball game.
>
> "When all a person's relevant skills are needed to cope with the challenges of a situation, that person's attention is completely absorbed by the activity. There is no excess psychic energy left over to process any information but what the activity offers. All the

attention is concentrated on the relevant stimuli.

"As a result, one of the most universal and distinctive features of optimal experience takes place: People become so involved in what they are doing that the activity becomes spontaneous, almost automatic; they stop being aware of themselves as separate from the actions they are performing."[27]

In the context of this type of activity, passion begins to appear in far greater supply; one's zeal for living, in general, naturally compounds as a by-product of the accumulation of these "free" moments. Life starts to get fun, and somewhere in there you actually begin to love it. Along the way, you typically notice that being "in the moment" also means that your automatic thinking—the "thousand screaming monkeys" in your head—has at long last quieted down. This, too, contributes greatly to your growing enjoyment of life.

Although activity ought not be relied upon as an escape from one's self, it proves an effective ticket to the experience of "flow." By coupling impassioned activity with mindfulness practice (meditation's "non-doing" path to flow), we have truly begun to cover all our happiness bases.

~~~

The words "passion" and "enthusiasm," for the sake of this discussion, mean pretty much the same thing: a zest for life or, at the very least, for that specific task in which you are presently engaged. The word "enthusiasm" comes from the Greek, "enthousiasmos," meaning "possession by God," "having a God within," or perhaps most literally, "in God." Reestablishing a connection to your enthusiasm, therefore, would seem essential for a return to "grace," "wholeness," "belonging," and to those elusive, castle-in-the-clouds-like states of "flow" and "well-being."

All these are your divine gifts, though you don't need to be "religious" or "spiritual" to feel any of them. You will, however, need to tap into your universal aspect in order to evolve beyond the mundane. Once in the Here and Now, the cultivation of what you want can begin in earnest. We already know that a consistent focus on your goal will not only help you achieve Csikszentmihalyi's optimal experience, but will also help you see through the maze of potential obstacles. This is what had occurred in my early "accidental" successes. With this in mind, you will want to spend some imagination time, at least twenty minutes every day, out in the warm, windy fields of your potential. There, in the serenity of your meditation or quiet relaxation time, you can fully drink in the imagined benefits of your win, already enjoying the *attainment* of what you, in your current physical reality, still have yet to realize.

These imagination fueled "thought seeds" will find extremely fertile ground in the alpha-level consciousness of meditation, so I do advise you to develop some sort of relaxation technique. This, essentially, becomes a powerful form of self-hypnosis, generating the inner shift wherein equivalent or complementary outer life-conditions can find their genesis.

Einstein understood the benefit of remaining close to his dream state. He would sleep no more than an hour and a half at a time, appreciating as he did the significant increase in creativity when in proximity to "alpha" and his dreaming consciousness.

~~~

Getting things to be "real" inside you in the face of physical evidence to the contrary can indeed be challenging. You will need to keep reminding yourself over and over again "what hinges upon what"—that life works sort of inside out—as your doubts begin to vie for your belief energy. Learning the sequence that creation *must* follow will help you to accept the possibility of getting what you want—even in the face of great doubt. For knowing that "belief," or mind energy, is always antecedent to that which is manifest will help you set your mind at ease as you start arguing with yourself about what is and isn't "true" or possible.

-47-   Zero Degrees Of Separation: Mystic Secret 11

Haiku—1984
I see me in your eyes.
I am you in disguise.

G. Rose

If it is true that All is One, and that All is Energy, and that Mind sets energy in motion, you ought to be able to tap into this Universal Mind for the sake of growing, changing, creating, and healing . . . all sorts of reality altering tasks. Let's try an exercise that will bring you closer to a mastery of this.

Exercise 11: You will need to find a quiet room. Remove all distractions (unplug the phone and close the door). Now sit in your favorite chair, get comfortable, and relax. Close your eyes and begin to focus your attention on your breath. This will help you quiet your thoughts.

Once you are relaxed, I want you to use your imagination like you did in Exercise 10—deliberately and as a tool. This time, however, I want you to conjure the image of someone you respect. This might be a teacher, a friend, or anyone who you truly admire. It might be a religious figure such as Christ, Buddha, or your minister or rabbi. You could have this person join you in a peaceful, remote setting, or he or she could appear standing or sitting opposite you in the very room in which you are now.

Look into his or her face. Feel what it feels like to be in this person's presence. Bask in it, and as you do, let yourself assume his or her energy. **Feel what you imagine it feels like to be him or her.** Trust that you have the ability to do this, and relax into the sensation. Don't get discouraged if this takes you a little time, it will be well worth it.

Spend approximately twenty minutes relaxing and experiencing the new energy. If you have difficulty with this, try changing the setting in which your encounter is taking place, or possibly switch to another respected individual. Then try it again. You may want to do this exercise using as many different people you admire as possible, for each may represent a different latent energy, talent, or character trait lying dormant within you. Give each a little time. You are working new muscles, and the sensations may feel strange to you at first.

Every time you complete this exercise, you will want to ask yourself, "Did I feel anything new—any new sensibilities or insights? If so, do these relate to 'quiet' qualities or ideas that already have a home in me?" Finally, ask yourself how you might realistically amplify or act upon these in the future.

~~~

This ability of yours to vicariously enjoy the qualities of others is one you know well; you have just never used it as a tool for growing. Our movie stars, sports heroes, and singing sensations all personify and magnify our own latent urges and undeveloped talents. The resonance, the sympathetic vibration that they set up, and that we feel in their presence, is why we idolize them. They allow us to feel, to brave, to explore, to break our own rules, and to do all this from the comfort of our couches. Lost in imagination, our deepest desires take flight, and for one brief shining moment, we "live" them.

Use this talent of yours to do more than just dream. Let it

wake within you the superstar that you are. And, as John Lennon so beautifully put it, "We'll all shine on, like the moon and the stars up above. On and on . . . ."

~~~

Since thought energy (thinking, imagining) precedes both feeling and manifestation (the creation of anything new), any shift, be it emotional or physical, will first require a shift in *intent*—the measure of your predominant thought. When you practice using your imagination to emulate the energy of those more evolved than you, it will help you awaken and "live" in any mutual possibilities and potentials that now sleep within you.

Once experienced, you have essentially spirited this potential from the realm of the impossible. For until you have sensed something for yourself, it is not real to you and, therefore, not possible *for* you. Repetition will make creating these new inner conditions easier and easier, which, in turn, will facilitate and insure the attraction of what, *energetically*, you now say you are ready to accept.

Practice this exercise every day for at least a month, or until it ceases to feel foreign and begins to fill you with delight. In a short time, it will become a place to which you look forward to going. At that point, do the exercise as often as you wish. This imagination-fueled state of awareness will be an important key to allowing yourself new possibilities. You can actually grow previously uncultivated personal aspects through association with those who are currently more developed than you.

Tennis players, ever notice that you play an increasingly better game of tennis the better your opponent? This is no coincidence.

-48-　Applied Thought Farming

In order to put the secrets of Thought Farming to work for you most effectively, you will first need to create a brand new condition *within* yourself; it must be a state wherein you value possibility more highly than familiarity. The exercises in this book can help you attain this new inner posture. Do yourself the first of a lifetime of important personal favors and work your way through them all. These exercises are designed to save you years of self-sabotaging and water treading.

It is through the reading and probably the re-reading of this material, and the doing of the exercises, that you will finally become the master of your fate and the captain of your soul. You will at long last learn how to work your own magic, by putting into practice what has, since your earliest childhood memories, been teasing you from the pages of your fairy tale books. Maybe you will "fly" like Peter Pan, or find your prince like Cinderella, or discover your very own Golden Goose. Whatever your desires may be . . . welcome home Thought Farmer. Welcome to a life of self-determination.

~~~

When René Descartes, seventeenth century French philosopher, said, "I think, therefore I am," it is not likely that he meant it from the practical standpoint of an industrious Thought Farmer. His meaning might possibly have been more along the lines, "I think, therefore I exist." That's O.K., we will reinvent him, too.

Theoretically, Thought Farmers believe that whatever we give sufficient thought energy or intention to, we become or draw into our lives—"I think, therefore I am." That will be the case if we are not cross-canceling our intent somehow by putting it out-of-phase through a subconscious body/mind posture. The "secrets" shared and exercises offered herein are designed to help you find and correct any such counter-productive position.

Once free of interference, you may leave the de-constructive phase behind and begin the practical application of what you have learned here. That is, to create entirely new conditions for yourself, be they in the area of health, personal life, or career. When you have done your preliminary work well, you will no longer be busy with hampering your own efforts, at least not full-time. Because of this, creating new conditions and experiences for yourself will be far easier than ever before.

~~~

Creation takes its cue from imagination, intention, and an unbridled subjective sense of "I can do that." To harness your personal power, you will need to give your meditations a dual purpose. The first ten minutes or so could be considered stress management time, where you simply float effortlessly and undirected—reducing any accumulated stress. When you are good and relaxed, you are most likely in or approaching an alpha brain-wave state; this is the perfect "season" to plant some new belief seeds.

Assuming that you have sufficiently Emotionally Detoxxed your subconscious, you will not have to spend an inordinate amount of time fending off doubt and disbelief. Therefore, once relaxed, you will be free to mentally conjure the experience or condition you wish to bring into physical form. In your self-guided fantasy, be as descriptive as you can. Incorporate as many details into the image of what you say you want as you can summon. The important thing here is that you fully enjoy your inner-vision. Let it take you to all sorts of pleasant new "exotic" interior energies. These sojourns may yield experiences of joy, love, success, freedom, health, wealth, friendship, or any one of countless other possible *positive* experiential destinations.

Suspend any remaining disbelief "stragglers" long enough to go *all the way* with your fantasy. Gently release your limiting thoughts as quickly as you can. In order to successfully Thought Farm, you have to be convinced—for at least the fifteen or twenty minutes that you are running your fantasy "movie"—that what you are imagining is actually true for you *now*. Then, during the day and evening, you may want to occasionally remind yourself of the positive experiences you earlier enjoyed.

But never argue about it with yourself. Spend no time trying to convince yourself of *anything*—neither the merits of the work nor the "truth" of the fantasy. Convincing always backfires, because it inadvertently sends the message, "I really don't believe this." If you can't revisit the earlier sensation without back talk from the peanut gallery, it's best not to try to do it at all.

Bedtime is a great time to do your imagination work. By giving yourself the equivalent of a self-hypnotic suggestion just before you doze off, you allow your dream consciousness to run with it throughout the night. You may then utilize your sleeping hours constructively. Oftentimes, you will wake to new ideas and insights that could have eluded you for days, weeks, months, or even years. If you are unhappy with the momentum this work is providing you, you will want to go back and re-do the Exercises. You likely have overlooked some of your "weeds," or they may have had deeper roots than first imagined. You may also want to revisit the discussions on imagination and on "letting-go."

Additionally, you will need to practice your muscle testing and Emotional Detoxx work. I think you will find that, at least for a while, you will have to keep accessing, experiencing, and renegotiating your nonbeneficial subconscious beliefs.

Let *The Truth and the Lie Game* help you achieve a new perspective on the more tenacious of these.

~~~

Stay with the same fantasy/goal for at least four to six weeks. Don't bounce all over the field imagining all sorts of different successes. You may, however, change the visuals surrounding your initial goal as often as you like. Just remember, *it's the feeling of "acquisition" that you are after.* The target in these energetic retreats is to experience the "win" that you seek as completely as possible. Then, relax the new idea and go about your business.

Over the course of the next month or so, you will want to keep your eyes, ears, and mind open to any Life-messages that may be responding to you. I can assure you that if you do this work properly, the universe *will* come back to you with Its response. You will have to learn, however, to recognize the various languages that It speaks. Answers may come quietly, subtly, in the form of off-handed, seemingly unimportant remarks; or they could hit you over the head like epiphanies. The more that you hone and develop your new inner awareness, the more likely it will be that you will start to recognize its corresponding forms within the world.

~~~

Once you have been "answered"—be it in the form of an idea, a dream, a newspaper article, something you see on TV, a friend's comment or suggestion, or an outright full-blown offering of your fantasy come-to-life—your follow-through will make or break your getting to keep it. You may remember the story of my deal with God, and how I subsequently met my friend who told me about the healer she had seen. In order to take advantage of the universe's reply to me, I needed to stay aware and be dedicated enough to connect the dots. I needed to recognize the health improvement in my friend and put it together with my own health fantasies. I needed to follow up and contact Stephanie, to make my desires known verbally, and to keep saying "yes" to all the new information that was pouring in on me.

~~~

There is a story about a priest who is caught in a flood. As the waters rise, a boat comes to his door. "Jump in," the people in the boat yell to the priest. The priest answers back, "Go my children, save yourselves. God will save me." An hour later, the waters have risen considerably, and the preacher climbs up to the roof of his house. Another boat comes by, and again he is beckoned on board. Stubbornly he waves them off, repeating, "Go my children, save yourselves. God will save me."

Soon the waters have risen so high that the priest is neck-up in river. A helicopter spots him and lowers a rope. But the priest does not grab the rope. Again, he insists, "Go my children, save yourselves. God will save me." Well, to make a long story short, the priest drowns. And as he stands before God in heaven, he asks, "Lord, why didn't you save me?" God looks at the saddened, perplexed man-of-the-cloth and says, "What are you talking about, my son? I sent you two boats and a helicopter."

We must learn to recognize the answers we seek, in all their myriad forms.

~~~

Remember, no dream is too extravagant, no thinking too wishful. Men and women have been manifesting extraordinary creations for centuries—scientists, inventors, artists, musicians, writers, architects, philosophers, political thinkers, and spiritual leaders. The list goes on and on.

Successful people are people who think differently than the majority. Because of this, they typically are considered a bit eccentric, but this does not stop them. Possibility *always* exceeds one's current reach. It takes vision, dedication, and a willingness to entertain new ideas, to reach for the seemingly impossible, and finally hold it in your hands. Don't be fooled by appearances. Just because you have no wings does not mean that you cannot fly. Just because you were not born privileged does not mean that you cannot have what you desire.

Most successful, joyful people were not simply handed "the good life" on a silver platter—they had to create it. The only real difference between you and them is that they kept an open mind and didn't let anything stop their progress. Look and listen for the answers you seek with openness. Weed your mind garden. Plant your new idea crops. Harvest your new conditions. Become a conscientious Thought Farmer. Recover, reunify, and release yourself, and take your place alongside the growing number of spirited self-made men and women of the world who understand and utilize the secrets of Thought Farming.

Mystic Secret 12: You realize that you are God in disguise the very moment that you no longer need to pretend to be someone else. Everything in creation is *in* God and *of* God. If you judge, resist, and limit that which you essentially are, you are no better than the Wizard is from *The Wizard Of Oz.* You are simply hiding behind your own inner walls and curtains. When you assume that you, exactly as created, are not good enough and refuse to be yourself, then try as you may, you will never be anything more than an imposter. To be or not to be is, indeed, the question.

It's a shame that the word "impulsive" has earned such a negative connotation. I believe this is because "impulse" appears to circumvent the analytical process that we, as a soul-starved society, have falsely, and much to our detriment, come to deify.

But *The Oxford Dictionary of English Etymology*, perhaps *the* most comprehensive etymological dictionary of the English language, defines "impulse" as the "act of impelling; *stimulation of the mind.*" And "impulsive" as "impelling to action; actuated by impulse." To act in accordance with the stimulation *of* the mind (not the manipulation *by* the mind) sounds to me like flow, sounds like integrity, sounds responsible, sounds as close as action is likely to get to Oneness, to spontaneous divine expression . . . sounds pretty darn good to me. Of course, I am talking about "clean" impulse, one not compensatory in any way. This mode of behavior must, therefore, be reserved only for the advanced Thought Farmer. Hence, this eleventh-hour suggestion: *If you are God, then you are good. Don't second-guess yourself.*

Exercise 12: Begin to say "Why not" when you are tempted to say "Why bother." Start saying "I will" where you habitually say "I shouldn't" or "I can't." Challenge, *through activity,* your fears and doubts. See if approaching yourself and your situations in ways previously summarily dismissed yields greater benefit to you. Experiment with your experience.

As you continue your release work—as you incorporate *The Truth and the Lie Game* and The Emotional Detoxx into your life, as you meditate, as you "let go" more and more, and as you flex your imagination muscles—saying "yes" will become easier and easier. You never know where a "yes" might lead. You know only too well where a "no" gets you.

When you have an idea, try acting on it as immediately as possible. Don't limit the nature or scope of this exercise. If you think to yourself, "The dishes need washing," then say "yes" and wash them. If you think of a friend out of the clear blue, call them that day if possible. If you have an idea to do something—whether it's an activity that, in the back of your mind, you have been wanting to do for a long time, or a brand new thought—don't talk yourself out of it. *Act.* Say, "Why not?" See what choosing "Yes," and then following through, could mean to you.

Choices are like New York City buses. You might have to transfer from one to another, and then maybe even to a third, before you get to where you want to go. Though the first bus may not be the one that ultimately gets you where you are going, if you don't get on it you will never get *anywhere.* Make a choice—say "yes"—get on the bus. You can always take a transfer.

Common Ground, Fertile Ground

Though very personal work, Thought Farming, if it is to have ongoing value, must ultimately include the whole in its private concerns. It is difficult, if not impossible, for an individual to have lasting health, wealth, or happiness in an ailing community. Conversely, no group can truly thrive if its members are still wrestling with the basics of survival. Therefore, Thought Farming, though firstly an "I" industry, must finally include a sensibility of "We."

Unfortunately, ever since the Enlightenment, the modern world has been reduced to an "It" culture. From this point on, if something could not be measured, quantified, put on a grid, and pointed to in some empirical way, it was simply not considered "real." Man's relationship with himself and his humanity were greatly affected by this "scientific" approach. Psychology would orphan the very highest aspect of the Mind, the "soul," what I call "I-ness," declaring these unreal, and therefore less worthy of proper scientific study. But the Mind is real, though it is real in ways different than the brain is real. Consequently, the study of Mind requires its own science, where each person becomes a scientist in his or her own personal laboratory, and where clinical results are always, inescapably, in the form of personal experience.

In the area of scientific investigation, an idea is considered hypothetical until someone or some team gathers enough statistical evidence so as to then call their theoretical notion "clinically proven." This determination can be made only after obtaining similar results time and time again, using identical or near identical conditions and technology. Basically, one wants to show that he or she has discovered or uncovered an essential "truth," wherein regardless of whose hands the pieces lie in, the puzzle will turn out looking the same.

The basic lesson of Thought Farming on the other hand, is that it is specifically *by virtue* of whose hands the pieces lie in that the puzzle takes shape. Even if every "player" is given exactly the same "pieces," no two puzzles will ever end up looking exactly the same. This is because the conditions—in this case, each person's *inner* condition—can never be fully reproducible.

The reason the rules seem to change for Thought Farming is that here *all* our results fit the "truths" of our beliefs. Results are, in fact, the very "truth" of our most deeply held beliefs. As scientific Thought Farmers, we must be willing to say "no" to a belief that yields unsatisfactory results, and "yes" to a belief imbued with the "truth" of a more favorable return. We do not ignore physical evidence; we are simply aware of the greater Truth that underlies that evidence.

We are no longer dealing with hard physical science, but rather with the invisible world that gives birth to that physical one—what more accurately must be called metaphysical or "soft science." Here, we do not escape the need for empirical evidence; we are simply operating in an area where the variables accounting for most of the observable differences are invisible, ephemeral, subconscious, subjective, and context dependent. Therefore, the causal factors are open to interpretation—making them harder to control and harder to identify.

~~~

For instance, take two children—from the same family; let's

make them identical twins, shall we—and let's raise them under conditions that are as identical as humanly possible. Regardless of our care, almost immediately and quite inevitably, divergent personalities begin to emerge. At this point, hard science would start looking for the causal variables responsible for the apparent forks created in what was ostensibly, certainly genetically, a mutual evolutionary road. But little to which it could put a yardstick would account for the great dissimilarities now beginning to emerge between Baby A and Baby B.

Nevertheless, one immediately encounters enormous difference that will have to be accounted for. One twin is outgoing, the other shy. One is terribly asthmatic, the other asthma-free. One has an artist's eye and hand, the other more mechanically inclined. One makes excellent grades in school, the other only average . . . etc, etc, etc. Hard science is hard pressed to find reasons for these dramatic differences; whereas Thought Farming, as a "soft" science, has only just "popped the hood" on the mechanics of creation and the infinite number of invisible variables potentially giving form to the emerging idiosyncrasies.

Within the world of the Thought Farmer, any change in intent or interpretation will inevitably yield a corresponding change in the observable results—the invisible becoming visible in accordance with one's subjective nature. We must, therefore, not only look at the empirical evidence, but at the inner world of meaning and intent that gives rise to that "truth." Because each twin in the above example has his or her own inner world—to the extent that this dimension exerts control over the act of creation (much)—they are not twins at all, but rather discrete, uniquely creative beings.

~~~

Thought Farming is based on the premise that an individual's creative ability, meaning his ability to create either health or ill-health, success or limited success, happiness or unhappiness—or for that matter any life experience at all—is dependent upon the immutable condition that he is an outpost of a common universal source Energy. As such, his creative potential will be dependent upon the degree to which he has given consent, either consciously or unconsciously, to be a conduit for this infinite resource.

Think about how much your fears and complaints distance you from Source. One of the things you probably don't like most about the people you don't care for is the amount of complaining that they do—those irritating fears and weaknesses reminding you of your own sense of separateness. What if you could remove all self-imposed limitation due to your lost sense of union, all the obstacles like fear, guilt, and anger that have become so precious to you? Well, you'd be able to see and to celebrate your unique and limitless potential, reveling in the responsibility you would then accept for everything which you create in your life. If we could all do this, we would all be much more likeable, though no more "alike." For each of us would still be a reflection of infinite Source—individually personified. Each of us, happily and completely taking control of his or her own personal universe and destiny.

Sure, we would still want to distinguish ourselves and competition would undoubtedly exist. But perhaps it would exist with a spiritual twist—one that could be an exercise in Unity, to see who might offer the greatest benefit to the common good. Barbara Marx Hubbard paints a fascinating picture of just such a future in *Conscious Evolution, Awakening the Power of Our Social Potential.*

~ ~ ~

Style is another way we have found to distinguish ourselves. In addition to the counseling work that I do, I have been active in the creative arts for many years as a writer and music producer. One of the more fascinating truths that I have discovered along the creative path is that "style"—the mark of individual expression—is primarily a function of *limitation*. In other words, when I encounter great skill, it normally accompanies less style than when I meet less talent that has needed to develop itself more pointedly—along a more finite, more narrowly defined artistic path.

Some talent is always necessary for good communication—musical or otherwise. But style seems to hinge upon *narrowing* the field of possible expression—hence, making the "artist" (the "individual voice" we seem to value so greatly). In contrast, the greater talent—displaying more expressive ability—makes for the "technician," whose style is not nearly so well-defined, owing to his or her use of a more limitless palette of expression. Of course, style could be a deliberate choice to limit or exaggerate within a fully developed talent. In my experience, however, this is not typically the case.

~ ~ ~

In life, too, much of what we consider to be "personality," "individuality," and "style" is actually only the result of our having narrowed the field of expression, resisting our limitless potential—the wide range that is always available to us by virtue of our connection to infinite Source. This is not to say that if we were all to suddenly get out of our own way and, in unison, hit divine stride, that there would be no idiosyncratic behavior or independent thought left in the world. I am certain that there would be. But the nature of that world would be far different than the one in which we currently live.

Yes, there would still be Yin and Yang, creation and discretion, life, death, love, happy and less happy, favorable and unfavorable conditions. But our uniqueness, our individual response to life would, in this handsome hypothetical, exclusively reflect those aspects of the universal that we each individually personify and would no longer *primarily* be a function of limitation.

There would, therefore, be no hate, no prejudice, no disease, no war and, mercifully, *no more complaining*. All these are merely a disguised reaction to fear, anger, guilt, or some other repressed emotion—which, by this point, would all be neatly handled healthfully, appropriately, and in a timely manner.

~ ~ ~

There is one more bit of "letting go" you will probably need to do if you are to find your universal Self. This involves your fear of "sameness." Leave it to an identical twin to figure out the importance of this one. Let's stop using our immature narcissistic need for distinction, style, or image as an excuse for remaining unevolved. You want style, great. Let it be the icing on your fully baked, Self-actualized cake. But for God's sake, for your sake, and for the sake of everything you hold dear, don't let style *be* the cake.

If you and I need to dig a little deeper, if we need to gaze a little longer down into our individual fathomless pools, down to where we intersect the infinite, and brave our similarities so that we may finally recover our lost natural euphoria and hidden creative ability, then so be it. After all, we are each made in the image and likeness of the very same "Thing" in the first place— that being God or universal Source. This, I'd say, is not too shabby a place to energetically meet.

Remember, the word "enthusiasm" literally means "in God." It would follow, then, that by turning within—toward our limitless, divine common ground—that it is here we could expect to find our lost enthusiasm. You do not have to die in order to return to

God. You do not have to become a religious fanatic or give away all your worldly possessions and live celibate on a mountaintop somewhere.

But you *will* have to do your best to kill off your limited, prejudicial thinking, to banish forever certain symbols from your vocabulary—words such as "right," "wrong," "good," "bad," "should," and "shouldn't." When you can accomplish this, you will be well on the way to living that fairy tale-like life of inclusion, represented by my idyllic farm portrait, wherein all things have their natural, rightful place . . . and *you* do, too.

Becoming self-referential will mean there can be neither comparison nor judgment. There can be no shame, there can be no guilt, and there can be no hate. Without comparison and judgment, there is no resistance to healthy feelings of anger, sorrow, fear or, for that matter, joy. Eden slowly begins to reemerge out from the primordial mist, and we at long last find ourselves back in the garden—back in grace. It is here that we may finally be that which we were intended to be: pristine points of awareness; unencumbered, joyful, creative beings; individual emanations of the One; Thought Farmers *par excellence*.

-50- | You Are the Farm

Bottom line, the way that you live your life is up to you. Society will do its utmost to convince you otherwise. Mother, father, boyfriend, girlfriend, husband, wife, child, religion, government, teacher, boss, client—all will make their agendas known to you in no uncertain terms. That's just the way life is.

First, however, you have a responsibility to yourself. Because if you don't take care of you, and subsequently fall apart, you won't be any good to yourself or to those who really must count on you. Much like the procedure for using emergency oxygen masks on an airplane, you have got to get yours on first, then you can help those around you.

You *are* the farm, and how you feel (by virtue of your total mind/body/soul experience) gives you the lay of the land. So keep your eye on the "map." What map is that? The one within you. The one that lets you know when something feels beneficial to you or not. This is not one of those old-fashioned, static, representative model types of maps that science is so fond of. This map is a living reflection—in *feeling*—of your evolutionary state. It is constantly changing, energetically morphing with each new bit of input. You read it by enhancing your awareness and discerning between that which feels beneficial or "good" to you, and that which does not.

By "beneficial" or "good," I do not mean a fleeting, transitory, euphoric "hit." Rather, I'm referring to a lasting, undeniable sense of having done something right for yourself, for someone else, and/or, in some way, for the world-at-large.

Let's call this the feeling of *grace*. If something seems *non-beneficial*, therefore, it wouldn't necessarily feel that way simply because it had made you feel guilty in the traditional sense, or because it had made someone else angry with you. Instead it would be nonbeneficial in a way where you sense—through a heart-centered awareness— that you had perpetrated some type of an injustice, either against yourself or another.

~~~

Watch out for guilt-wielding parents; they are deadly experts at jumbling our inner compasses. Gaining facility in sorting through guilt feelings can take many years. Maintaining rationality while jumping through hoops is a trick that requires much practice. A good start would be to assume that if something you think, do, or say feels "bad" to you, it should be examined, challenged, and possibly reevaluated. If something feels "good" and seems to unjustly hurt no one, you would do well to give yourself permission to think it, do it, or say it more often. This is not a perfectly foolproof system, but it's a good beginning. No outside standards can be used. No one else will ever be able to tell you whether you are right or wrong. That is between you and the divine sense of balance within you.

Any thought or action that contradicts a healthy "good" feeling is generally guilt-driven. Here I am not referring to Seth's "natural guilt," as discussed earlier in Chapter Seventeen, which is actually a great map reading device. Nor am I speaking about conscience. Guilt sabotages all efforts at happiness by putting someone else's "X" on your map, where it couldn't possibly belong, and where you have absolutely no hope of ever finding it. **Guilt is always bad counsel. It is an other-oriented emotion meant to serve someone else.**

Of course, society has its rules and its laws. If we break these, we will be subject to whatever punishment it deems fitting. But our judicial system, powerful as it is, has no jurisdiction over our hearts, nor does it have dominion over the immutable Laws by which the universe itself is governed.

In terms of life's treasure, the "X" on your map, that place offering you the greatest personal reward, does indeed "mark the spot." The reason choice must ultimately remain very personal is that no one but *you* can get inside you to determine where your "X" is. Only you will know when something feels right. Only you will remember by what "tree" or under what "rock" you have hidden your exuberance, your passions, and your lost childhood ecstasy.

~~~

Speaking of ecstasy, you will find that a successful Thought Farmer will tend to smile a great deal. This is because he has been very discriminating as to what sort of energy "seeds" he has scattered across his fields. How did he know which to choose? He consulted his map.

The very act of entertaining a choice has an energetic consequence, a feeling associated with it. Making the choice has further consequences. The action required to support that choice, again, will bring experiential consequences. And finally, the result of that action will exhibit consequences of its own. All these stages have some sort of experience attached to them.

From a well nurtured, clean choice-field, you would, moment-by-moment, acknowledge your degree of enjoyment or displeasure. Having Emotionally Detoxxed, you will be virtually free of historical context. Squarely in the Here and Now, you would simply opt for that which afforded you the most favorable feelings and move on to your next choice (Seth's "natural guilt"). You would routinely select the more life-enhancing sensations for two important reasons. One, they feel better; and two, your newly established status quo would insist upon it. For the now greater familiarity with these "positive" feelings would deem them the most real to you. In the past—when your more intimate acquaintance was with painful limiting beliefs and feelings—*those* seemed more real.

Until you are more familiar with pleasant rather than unpleasant sensation, this process may remain challenging for you. This is why you will want to learn the secrets of Thought Farming and review them often, and why you will want to do the exercises presented throughout these pages. You are changing horses mid-stream, and the current can get mighty rough at times. Persevere, and you are going to make it. Just don't give up.

Perseverance, herein, asks that every step of the way, moment-by-moment, you consult and give credence to your inner map. You will want to "take a reading" to see what your body "feels," what your mind "thinks," and what your spirit "senses."

The words "success" and "successful" have the same root as the word "succession." "Succession" means a series of steps—putting one foot in front of the other. You *will* have success if you just keep your map handy. If you learn to trust it and use it step-by-step, choice-by-choice, the road home won't feel nearly so long. Then, as you continue to search your inner ground for your "bread crumb clues"—those feelings that you left scattered behind you so long ago—the "hole in your soul" will begin to mend. Soon your heart will lighten and again fill with hope.

Once homeward, it is only a matter of time before you *are* home. Here, at the end of an inner pilgrimage that has seen you return to the true promised land—your Actual-Self—you will turn in, deservedly weary, close your eyes, and sleep the sleep of angels. When the morning comes, you will rise, laugh at the damn "rooster" and, in the peace that comes from listening to your own heart, begin at long last to work *your* farm *your* way. This time in the dawn of a very brand new day.

Are those cinnamon rolls I smell?

Epilogue | "G." Whiz! This Stuff Really Works.

G. That's me. One final case history . . . .

Over the course of writing *When You Reach The End Of Your Rope, Let Go!*, I, too, have been in process. I had been preparing for the next big step in my life—to find my life partner. I was married once before, to an incredibly lovely woman who taught me about loving and giving. But my relationship with my ex-wife proved more mother/son than man/woman. I had met Bobbi in my late teens, when she was infinitely more developed than I. For that reason, and for reasons relating to what she needed for herself at the time, we forged a loving, albeit doomed relationship. Eighteen years on, we finally grew apart, threw in the proverbial towel, and divorced. On a happier note, she remains one of my closest friends to this day.

In the years that followed, I had not succeeded in finding a suitable mate. I knew it was because there was some resistance within me that needed unearthing and releasing. Using every tool I have presented to you, I started "cleaning house" again. The writing of *When You Reach . . .* was the perfect vehicle for this work, in that it relentlessly reminded me of what I needed to be doing . . . Physician, heal thyself.

Toward the conclusion of my work on the book, and after several weeks of solitary introspection, I got the idea—and knew I had to follow through on it—to call a friend of mine, Cheryl Cummings, Ph.D., a holistic health practitioner. Unbeknownst to me (consciously), Cheryl was experimenting with some new energy work she called Holographic Repatterning™. Like the exercises presented herein, her work involved the retracing of resisted belief and feeling energy, and the releasing of this energy.

Instead of seeking the expression of what we uncovered through feeling alone, Cheryl employed color, smell, and sound as additional energy rebalancing agents. You see, everything is energy. Whether you and I use thought, feeling, sound, color, aromatherapy, or all of the above, we are simply treating energy *with* energy.

~~~

Like Stephanie Ewings, Cheryl Cummings understood this "everything is energy" notion. She knew that if I didn't have what I said I wanted, it was because I was still, in some important way, resisting it. To her thinking, and mine, there was an energetic block somewhere in my Body/Mind. Using muscle testing, we determined that there was, indeed, such a block directly related to my inability to create a life mate . . .

· *My unwillingness to "release the pain by releasing the tears"* was central to my mating problem.

Now, I've cried a lot of tears in my lifetime, so at first I was hesitant to accept our findings. But I believe everything that I have shared with you throughout these pages and have seen it work miracles time and again. So I was forced to take a closer look. Using the muscle testing, Cheryl and I delved further and deeper. Sure enough—early, early on, around the age of six months—I had resisted feelings of abandonment related to my biological father and my parents' early divorce. That made sense to me: mating problems *caused* by mating problems. Though I had never been aware of any pain associated with their separation— there it was, speaking from deep within me.

I gave myself permission to accept the possibility of having experienced just such pain—and then having recoiled from the intensity of it. When I did this, something stirred within me. Cheryl asked me to think of the color yellow and to sing the note A. Tears followed and a deep sorrow filled me. After a minute or two, the tears subsided, I regained my composure, and we retested. The energetic block was gone.

I am sure that a similar release could have been achieved through *any* core-level feeling work, but I needed to honor my thought about Cheryl, and enjoyed playing with her new tools.

Immediately following our session together, I went to a friends home where he was throwing himself a large house-warming party. Half-kiddingly, Cheryl's parting words to me were "Let me know if you meet someone there."

The gathering was fun, much like any other of its kind. And like other such parties, I saw no one who struck me as being particularly exciting. But I mingled just the same, while keeping an open mind and an open heart.

I still smelled like the rose oil, which Cheryl had me rub at my heart center at the conclusion of our session. Some of the guests were teasing me about it. It *was* kind of funny, actually. I smelled like a too heavily perfumed old lady. "Great," I said to myself, "this is *really* gonna help."

About an hour after arriving, I noticed a pretty woman speaking to a man and another woman. *She* looked promising. But they talked, and they talked, and they talked. I thought the conversation would never end. Finally, she briefly left the room, and upon returning, she handed the man one of her business cards. Great, I thought, she may be single.

They parted, at last, and the pretty woman miraculously made her way close to where I was standing. Her presence did not go unnoticed by me. As quickly as good manners would allow, I finished up the conversation I was having, and turned to introduce myself to her. With a soft but detectable accent she said her name was Alyson . . .

Aly was smart. *Great.* She was good-natured. *Wonderful.* She was beautiful. *Excellent.* She was engaging. *Delightful.* She was also petite, Scottish, and unattached. *Yes. Yes. Yes.*

Best of all . . . She had that sweet, intangible, X-factor. And, oh yeah, she seemed to like me, too.

After several minutes of getting-to-know-one-another, I jumped headlong into a *non sequitur* and asked if I could have her phone number. Aly smiled and left the room once more to fetch another business card. Meanwhile I thought to myself, "That other guy doesn't stand a chance." Now I'm not normally so cock-sure about these things. But Aly seemed a perfect energetic match to the woman I had been holding in my mind's eye all these years. This was no coincidental meeting, I thought. This was creation at its divine best—I was certain of it.

When she returned and handed me her card, Aly said that she didn't really know why she was doing it, because she had recently finalized plans to leave the country and return to her native Scotland within the month. My heart sank. I'm sure I was visibly disappointed. But I stayed true to my intuition, took the card, and told her that I would call her anyway, deciding that stranger things than this have happened on the rocky road to love. "Just a bump," I comforted myself. "Just a bump."

~~~

Before our first date, I decided to take out an insurance policy by making one more deal with God. This time I told Him that I would accept any outcome that would most highly serve God-as-Aly, God-as-myself, and God-as-every-other-aspect-of-creation. If she *were* my life partner, these *must* be the terms, anyway. Frankly, despite Aly's plans to leave the country, I still felt, somehow, that the deck was stacked in my favor. That the universe, unbeknownst to this beautiful being, had dealt me a winning hand.

Our first date went incredibly well, each of us sharing at

levels that created instant intimacy. From the hole-in-the-wall Mexican place where we had margaritas and a bite, to the all-night coffeehouse where we settled further into knowing each other, I sensed more and more that I was in the presence of a dream come true. At her door, at evening's end, I asked Aly if I could kiss her goodnight. She said yes. That kiss held the promise of eternity in its tender passion.

~ ~ ~

To make a tumultuously joyous, romantically whirlwindish, long story very short . . . We have since fallen deeply in love, Aly is *not* moving back to Scotland, and we are enjoying life together.

I had completed yet another arc. I had once again made "magic," by doing the inner work needed to pave the way for the universe to deliver me a brand new "reality." In its ever-mystical, mind-boggling way, Thought Farming had created another sweet, abundant harvest. Through the process of writing this book and, more importantly, trusting the information herein and "walking the walk," I had reached the end of yet another rope, had let go once more into the great unknown, and had once again bettered my life.

Just this morning, I thanked God, drafted this final chapter, and, of course, I cried.

The Beginning.

If you wish to contact the author, visit the Emotional Detoxx website at www.emotionaldetoxx.com

Bibliography

[1] Mark Epstein, M.D., *Thoughts Without a Thinker: Psychotherapy from a Buddhist Perspective* (New York, NY Basic Books, 1995), p. 173.

[2] Mark Epstein, M.D., *Thoughts Without a Thinker: Psychotherapy from a Buddhist Perspective* (New York, NY Basic Books, 1995), p. 48.

[3] William Elliot, *Tying Rocks to Clouds: Meetings and Conversations with Wise and Spiritual People* (New York, NY Doubleday, 1996), p. 63.

[4] Mihaly Csikszentmihalyi, *Flow, The Psychology of Optimal Experience* (New York, NY Harper Perennial, 1991), p. 120.

[5] Theresa Dale, Ph.D., N.D., *Transform Your Emotional DNA: "Understanding the Blueprint of Your Life"* (Los Angeles, CA The Wellness Center for Research and Education 1995 & 1996), p. 67.

[6] Robert A. Johnson, *He, Understanding Masculine Psychology, Revised Edition* (New York, NY Harper & Row, 1989), p. 56.

[7] Robert A. Johnson, *HE, Understanding Masculine Psychology, Revised Edition* (New York, NY Harper & Row, 1989), p. 70.

[8] Carolyn Myss, Ph.D., *Anatomy of the Spirit* (New York, NY Three Rivers Press, 1996) p. 132.

[9] Ken Wilber, *A Brief History of Everything* (Boston, MA Shambhala Publications Inc., 1996), p. 156.

[10] Dr. Irving Oyle, *The New American Medicine Show* (Santa Cruz, CA Unity Press, 1979), pp. 160, 163, 164.

[11] Mihaly Csikszentmihalyi, *Flow, The Psychology of Optimal Experience* (New York, NY Harper Perennial, 1991), p. 206.

[12] Marianne Williamson, *A Return To Love, Reflections on the Principles of "A Course in Miracles"* (New York, NY HarperCollins Publishers, 1994), p. 53.

[13] Howard Halpern, *Cutting Loose; An Adult's Guide to Coming to Terms with Your Parents* (New York, NY Simon & Schuster, 1976, 1990), p. 140.

[14] Mark Epstein, M.D., *Thoughts Without a Thinker: Psychotherapy from a Buddhist Perspective* (New York, NY Basic Books, 1995), Foreword.

[15] Howard Halpern, *Cutting Loose; An Adult's Guide to Coming to Terms with Your Parents* (New York, NY Simon & Schuster, 1976, 1990), p. 254.

[16] Harville Hendrix, Ph.D., *Getting the Love You Want, A Guide for Couples* (New York, NY Harper & Row, 1988, 1990), p. 281.

[17] Ernest Holmes, *Lessons in Spiritual Mind Healing* (Los Angeles, CA Science Of Mind Publications, 1943), p. 41.

[18] Andrew Weil, M.D., and Winifred Rosen, *From Chocolate to Morphine: Everything You Need to Know about Mind-Altering Drugs* (New York, NY Houghton Mifflin Company, 1993), p. 16.

[19] Andrew Weil, M.D., and Winifred Rosen, *From Chocolate to Morphine: Everything You Need to Know about Mind-Altering Drugs* (New York, NY Houghton Mifflin Company, 1993), p. 17.

[20] Dr. Irving Oyle, *The New American Medicine Show*, (Santa Cruz, CA Unity Press, 1979), p. xii.

[21] David Tame, *The Secret Power of Music, The Transformation of Self and Society through Musical Energy* (New York, NY

Destiny Books, 1984), p. 215.

[22] Ernest Holmes and Willis H. Kinnear, *A New Design for Living* (New York, NY Prentice Hall Press, 1987), p. 11.

[23] Ernest Holmes and Willis H. Kinnear, *A New Design for Living* (New York, NY Prentice Hall Press, 1987), p. 12.

[24] *The Mirriam Webster Dictionary* (Springfield, MA Mirriam Webster, Incorporated, 1994), p. 368.

[25] Shakti Gawain, *Creative Visualization* (New York, NY Bantam New Age Books, 1985), pp. 22–24.

[26] Ernest Holmes, *The Science of Mind* (New York, NY Dodd, Mead & Company, 1938), p. 399.

[27] Mihaly Csikszentmihalyi, *Flow, The Psychology of Optimal Experience* (New York, NY Harper Perennial, 1991), pp. 48, 53.